EDEN

Steve Carter

BROADWAY PLAY PUBLISHING INC
New York
www.broadwayplaypub.com
info@broadwayplaypub.com

Cover art by Paul Evan Jeffrey

First BPPI edition: August 2024
I S B N: 978-0-88145-898-5

Book design: Marie Donovan
Page make-up: Adobe InDesign
Typeface: Palatino

EDEN was first presented by The Negro Ensemble
Company at the Saint Marks Playhouse opening on 3
March 1976. The cast and creative contributors were:

EUSTACE BAYLOR.............................. Samm-Art Williams
NIMROD BARTON..Nate Ferrell
SOLOMON BARTON...................... Laurence Fishburne, III
LIZZIE HARRIS.................................Barbara Montgomery
AGNES BARTON .... Ramona King
ANNETTE BARTON .... Shirley Brown
FLORIE BARTON ....Ethel Ayler
MR JOSEPH BARTON .... Graham Brown

Director.................................... Edmund Cambridge
Stage Manager...............................Clinton Turner Davis
Sets.. Pamela S Peniston
Lighting...Sandra L Ross
Costumes... Edna Watson

EDEN subsequently transferred to the Theatre de Lys.

PUBLISHER'S NOTE

I first met Steve Carter in 1985 or 1986. In May of 1985, Broadway Play Publishing Inc published a collection, *Short Pieces from the New Dramatists*; Steve was a member of that wonderful playwrights' development organization then; that book had two of his plays in it. In January of 1986, his HOUSE OF SHADOWS was produced at The Negro Ensemble; BPPI published it in *Plays by Steve Carter* in December. His next play, in 1990, was PECONG, a MEDEA set in the West Indies, first produced at Victory Gardens in Chicago where he was part of their playwrighting group; that production later played at Newark Symphony Hall Second Floor Theater where I saw it (and then published it).

All of that was years after EDEN had first been produced (also by the Negro Ensemble) in 1976, before Broadway Play Publishing Inc even existed. EDEN was published that year but eventually went out of print. We are pleased to now have almost all of Steve's plays (he died in 2020 at the age of 90) at one publisher. His stage directions have been faithfully reproduced from the original edition with minimal conforming to the BPPI house style.

Christopher Gould

CHARACTERS & SETTING

EUSTACE BAYLOR
NIMROD BARTON
SOLOMON BARTON
LIZZIE HARRIS
AGNES BARTON
ANNETTE BARTON
FLORIE BARTON
MR JOSEPH BARTON

The action takes place on 63rd Street between 10th and 11th Avenues in Manhattan. This section was called San Juan Hill.

The time is August to December of 1927.

Dedicated to Ma…Toots…Stevie and Scott, and special thanks to Douglas Turner Ward.

ACT ONE

(A four unit set…consisting of an apartment, a hallway with a window and stairs leading up to a roof…and a working door to an apartment….)

(EUSTACE BAYLOR is sitting at the hallway window sketching on a large pad…. NIMROD BARTON is on the roof rolling up a ball of string from his home-made kite…. SOLOMON is in his apartment studying from his home-bound book. NIMROD comes down from the roof.)

EUSTACE: *(He turns in chair to NIMROD.)* Hi!

NIMROD: Hello.

EUSTACE: How you doin'?

NIMROD: Okay! You're always sketching.

EUSTACE: You always kite flyin'.

NIMROD: I like to fly kites.

EUSTACE: I like sketchin'!

NIMROD: What are you drawing?

EUSTACE: Er…nothing particular…street…people. Sure is a lotta people livin' on this one street….

NIMROD: *(Crosses right to window up stage of EUSTACE. Looks out. Sneaks a look at EUSTACE sketch.)* Where? I don't see a lot of people.

EUSTACE: Guess you just used to it…it bein' your city and all…things is easier in my home…folks spread out a bit…

NIMROD: Guess so. *(He crosses left to apartment door.)*

EUSTACE: You West Indian, ain't you?

NIMROD: What of it?

EUSTACE: Don't go puttin' yourself in no huff. I was just askin'…is all. Ain't never really knowed no West Indians before.…

NIMROD: Well…you know one now. As you can see we got two asses just like everybody else.…

EUSTACE: You sure don't talk like one.

NIMROD: What're we supposed to talk like…? Besides, I was born here.

EUSTACE: Oh, so you ain't…

NIMROD: …So it makes no difference. I'm still…

EUSTACE: Listen, you be what you wanna be. Don't make me no never mind. A nigger's a nigger.

NIMROD: I'm not a nigger.… *(He throws kite down, makes a fist and crosses right to* EUSTACE.*)*

EUSTACE: Look… *(He stands left of chair.)* I ain' been up here long. I don't wanna get started off on the wrong foot. So lemme see if I got this straight. Now, you say you was born here in these United States…but you's a West Indian. Your skin's the same color as mine…your hair is as burly as mine…but you ain't a nigger…guess it's me that's all mixed up…

*(*NIMROD *crosses to kite, picks up; crosses right to* EUSTACE. NIMROD *glares at* EUSTACE. EUSTACE *smiles back steadily. Realizing* NIMROD *is somewhat fired up,* EUSTACE *stands and stretches lazily letting his full height be seen.* EUSTACE *sits chair resumes sketching.)*

EUSTACE: Guess I'll be gettin' back to my sketchin'.
(NIMROD *enters apartment, crosses left.* SOLOMON *stage left chair at table.*)

NIMROD: Ain't you ready?...

SOLOMON: No!

NIMROD: *(He crosses left through arch enter down stage room. Leaves kite off stage)* Why 're you readin' that shit...?

SOLOMON: In case you've forgotten...he'll be home today and you know he'll be asking questions....

NIMROD: So? *(He enters crosses up stage to cabinet. Takes cookie box. Crosses down stage to up center table. Places cookie box)* Can't you fake the answers?

SOLOMON: No! And you don't do so good either! Why do you risk getting your ass torn up when it's just simpler to learn the stuff ?

NIMROD: Look...man. *(He opens box. Takes cookie)* It's summertime. We're supposed to be on school vacation...anyway, come on we have to go and pick up that shit...and I want to go and play down by the docks before we have to go to Mr Wallaces's store. *(He crosses to apartment door.)*

SOLOMON: Papa told us to stay away from the tracks.

NIMROD: *(He turns crosses up center table.)* Oh, shit...it's probably gonna be the last time. Now come on.... You can study that shit later. *(He crosses up right center to door, exits apartment, crosses up right. Exits down steps to street.)* ...Come on.

SOLOMON: Okay... *(He stands, takes cookie crosses to door...puts iron inside, closes door, crosses up right exits down steps to street.)*

(NIMROD *and* SOLOMON *leave the apartment and go downstairs.*)

LIZZIE: *(From within)* Eustace, where you?

(EUSTACE doesn't answer.)

LIZZIE: Eustace, where you at? *(To herself)* If that don't beat all. He got the dishes clean and *(She opens her door crosses to stairs, turns. Sees EUSTACE)* already, gone, Aha! ...There you.

EUSTACE: *(He brings head in window.)* What you want... Aunt Lizzie?

LIZZIE: Nothin' particular. See you already washed up all the dishes while I was nappin'. Keep tellin' you... You don't have to be doin' that. That's woman work. I'm supposed to be spoilin' you and here you turnin ' my head 'round.

EUSTACE: You never know how hard a woman work 'till you lose one. Hard work done took my mama. I ain't 'bout to 'low the only kin I got left to do no kinda hard work if I can help it. 'Sides, ain't nothin' to washin' no dishes.

LIZZIE: You sweet...boy! *(She crosses right to EUSTACE, hugs him.)* And you my sister for the world. You big like your daddy but you my sister for the world.

EUSTACE: Stop that or you gonna set yourself to cryin' again. She dead and I miss her more than fierce but I know she better off where she at. She don't feel no pain no more...and I expect she happy knowin' I'm up here with you...and if she happy...I'm happy.

LIZZIE: Go'n with you...how 'bout another piece of cobbler?

EUSTACE: 'Bout to bust now. Ain't been up here no time yet and you done fed me 'nough to 'splode a bear.

LIZZIE: Don't want my sister lookin' down and sayin' I ain't takin' care of her baby. *(She crosses into apartment gets chair and crosses into hall. Places chair left of EUSTACE.)*

She has brought a chair into the hall and placing it in front of her door, she makes herself at home.) Well, it sure ain't take you no time to pick up hallway habits. What's so interestin' out that window you can't see from inside the house...?

EUSTACE: Nothin'. Just cooler out here.

LIZZIE: Cooler, hunh?

EUSTACE: 'Sides, I just can't get used to seein' so many folks livin' on this one itty-bitty street.

LIZZIE: Guess we all sort of pop-eyed 'bout it when we first come up here, but you get used to it after a time. I don't pay it no 'tention no more.

EUSTACE: But you sure can see why people holdin' court in the hallway.

LIZZIE: In case you ain't noticed, it's only us decent folks can sit in the hall. Them folks that live up the other end of the street can't do it. It's nice to sit here outta the sun. You get the breeze...and all the news... never did hold with sittin' on the stoop. 'Sides them folks up the other end of the street got toilets in their halls...and no windows in 'em. Can you beat that? Lord...Lord when me and Anse first come up here... we live up there and, Lord...sometimes...I damn near wet myself not goin' to the toilet when I had to... just used to hate thinkin' 'bout performin' my body functions. I mean sometimes you had to wait in line... then you most times had to clean up behind somebody. Eustace, be glad we livin' in these here Phipps houses...we livin' good now. Four or five sets of strangers usin' the same convenience...disgustin'! *(She cuts short her memory.)* Anyway...what you drawin' this time?

EUSTACE: Nothin' particular. Just scratchin'.

LIZZIE: That's for sure the Lord's truth...and I know what you scratchin' after....

EUSTACE: Now, Aunt Lizzie.

LIZZIE: Don't, "now, Aunt Lizzie" me. You know I weren't born the seventh daughter of a seventh daugh ter for nothin'.

EUSTACE: You ain't no seventh daughter of no seventh daughter.

LIZZIE: Don't make no difference, I can still tell what you up to.

EUSTACE: Like I was glass...hunh ?

LIZZIE: See right through you. At any rate, you better stop sniffin' after who you sniffin' after. You ain't never been caught up with no strange niggers like them next door.

EUSTACE: They ain't so bad...and I thought you and Mrs Barton was friends....

LIZZIE: That's right...but you know I ain't never been in that house when that man was home. Sundays and holidays, I mean I even fix a plate for Mrs Barton to taste...and she likewise for me...but like I said...if he's there...I ain't.

EUSTACE: Can't be that bad....

LIZZIE: That West Indian ain't real...don't even blink... he be home from the hospital today and you see... tell me when that streetcar hit him his blood come out pure ice...he be home. Don't like none of us homeys... won't even talk to nobody unless they born cross the pond like him...hardly talk to more than a handful of them...I never seen that man walk nothin' but a straight line and folks pure get outta his way...that Indian nigger can walk straight up sixty third street 'cross tenth avenue right into little Ireland and none

of them Irish niggers ever bother him…and you tryin'
to mess with one of his daughters. The way that man
hang over them two…'specially the one you after…
you'd think they shit rose petals…pardon my french.…
Ain't you listenin' to me, boy? Bring your head in that
window.

EUSTACE: Aunt Lizzie… *(He stands crosses to* LIZZIE,
tries to lift her from chair.) she comin' down the street.…
Whyn 't you go'n inside?

LIZZIE: Boy if you ain't your father when it comes to
the ladies.…

EUSTACE: Never knew him…now be my angel and…

LIZZIE: Well I knew him…and you just him all over
again.

*(*EUSTACE *exits right into apartment with sketch book and
pencil.)*

LIZZIE: Lord…when that man made up his mind to
step some gals' way, couldn't nobody *(She stands
crosses right stands up stage side apartment door.)* man…
law or God stop him.… I was too through when his eye
lit on your mama. *(She crosses left leans on back left chair.)*

EUSTACE: Can't we talk on that some other time, Aunt
Lizzie? If you just worryin' bout her father…forget it.
(He crosses into hall buttoning shirt and tucking in pants.)
I ain't set on myself or nothin' like that but granny told
me once that couldn't nobody who see me fail to like
me…and maybe somebody like me is what the ol' man
need.…

LIZZIE: I say…be careful.…

EUSTACE: Ain't nobody gonna get hurt…I'm just out to
fun a little.…

LIZZIE: I don't wanna see that gal hurt. Lord knows…
there's enough gals hurtin' 'cause o' y'all men…but

sure as hell don't wanna see you hurt neither. ...You
and me is the last of the blood...who else you got 'to
look out for you...

EUSTACE: I can take care of myself...it's time you
know.... *(He crosses up stage to hall steps.)*

LIZZIE: I know you big...and you sure seen enough for
your age...

(LIZZIE stops EUSTACE.)

LIZZIE: Ain't nobody supposed to see their momma go
the way you did, but Eustace you still a baby far as this
world's concerned....

EUSTACE: I'm goin' downstairs now. You go'n inside.
Thanks for worryin' 'bout me. Don't never stop...but I
told you...I'm just funnin'! *(He exits up stage, exits down
steps to street.)* Just funnin'! *(He kisses her on the cheek and
goes downstairs.)*

LIZZIE: *(To herself)* You just your father... *(She takes left
chair crosses right, places it inside apartment. Then stands
in apartment door eavesdropping .)* all over again.

EUSTACE: *(From below)* Hello, mistress Agnes....
Mistress 'Netta. How you both today?

AGNES: *(From below and affecting a southern accent.)* Fine!
We both fine, thank you kindly! 'Scuse us, please!

EUSTACE: *(From below.)* 'Low me to help you with them
bags. Little ladies like yourselfs shouldn't have to heft
things like that up no stairs....

AGNES: *(From below.)* We don't mind "heffin". In fact,
we love to heft.

EUSTACE: I insist.

AGNES: Suit yourself.

*(AGNES gives EUSTACE two shopping bags. LIZZIE exits
right into apartment leaving door slightly ajar.)*

(AGNES *enters hall crosses left opens* BARTON *apartment door.* ANNETTA *gives* EUSTACE *shopping bag.*)

ANNETTA: Thank you.

EUSTACE: My pleasure…you sure got a lotta packages.

(AGNES *crosses up stage to hall steps.*)

AGNES: If they're too much for you…

(ANNETTA *appears top of steps in hall crosses down right center hall.*)

EUSTACE: I can handle 'em.

ANNETTA: I know you can. You 're big enough to carry a house.…

AGNES: Annetta!

ANNETTA: I'll bet you could too carry a house.

(EUSTACE *appears top hall step with three shopping bags crosses down center. They reach the landing.*)

AGNES: Thank you! *(She crosses right to* EUSTACE *takes two shopping bags.)* We'll take these now.

EUSTACE: We here already?

AGNES: It would seem so… *(She crosses left enters apartment crosses left to cabinet, places bags on floor. Puts groceries from one bag in oak cabinet, folds bag crosses up stage, places bag in grey sink cabinet.)*

EUSTACE: I should take these in for you.

ANNETTA: Oh, no. Thank you! I mean…

EUSTACE: I know you can't ask me in. Listen, it's good your daddy don 't want no fast talkin' galloots in the place when he ain't home. Some guys would take sore advantage of a little thing like you…I heard he coming home from the hospital today.

ANNETTA: My mother's gone to get him. That's why we've done all this shopping.

EUSTACE: A little celebration, hunh?

ANNETTA: Yes.

EUSTACE: I know you be glad to see him.

ANNETTA: Yes.

EUSTACE: I guessed you missed him a lot?

ANNETTA: Yes.

AGNES: *(She crosses to platform, props door open with iron.)* Annetta, are you coming in any time soon?

ANNETTA: *(She crosses left to* BARTON *doorway)* In a minute…or two.

AGNES: *(She props* BARTON *apartment door open with iron door stop.)* Dinner had better be ready when he comes. It's not me who's the so-called "best cook in the world".

ANNETTA: Since it's me, I wouldn't worry me head, Agnes dear.

*(*AGNES *crosses into up stage room takes bag to front cabinet. To* EUSTACE. ANNETTA *takes bag from* EUSTACE.*)*

ANNETTA: I do have to go.…

EUSTACE: Look like we ain't gonna have no time for no niceties.… Shoot, you eighteen…this is 1927. Shoot… girls back home durn near grandma's…your age.…

ANNETTA: Well…I'm sorry. *(She starts to enter apartment.)*

EUSTACE: Now, don't go gettin' in a pout. You West Indians sure is some quick to fire. Funnin ' with one of your brothers little bit ago and he look like he want to walk all over me.

ANNETTA: You know nothing of us…or me.

EUSTACE: I know your father don't like niggers, but shit.…

ANNETTA: Don't curse....

EUSTACE: I ain't say nothin' but "shit" ...and like I was sayin' I know your father don't like us niggers but all I wanna do is take you somewhere.

ANNETTA: Where?

EUSTACE: How I know? Somewhere! Anywhere, for a walk. Shit, somewhere! I wanna be seen with you....

ANNETTA: I have to go inside.

EUSTACE: Aw, c'mon, 'Netta. Like I said we ain't got too much time and I want to nail this down.

ANNETTA: Nail what down...?

EUSTACE: Okay I want you to go with me...and if you say, "where" I'll...well you ain't all that...I mean you ain't dumb.

ANNETTA: You don't really know me....

EUSTACE: Do, too...and wanna know you more... wanna know all about you. All I really know 'bout you now...is that ain't nobody from the bunch I seen around here good enough for you.

ANNETTA: And you are?

EUSTACE: No! I probably ain't good 'nough for you.... But I'm right for you and I 'spect you know that!

AGNES: *(She enters from up stage room crosses right to platform, with typing papers and folder and red pencil.)* Girl, papa and mama coming down the street.

ANNETTA: *(She crosses left into* BARTON *door, stands on platform.)* I have to go.

EUSTACE: *(He crosses left, stands in doorway.)* What's your answer?

AGNES: You're gonna get it!

ANNETTA: Please, we'll talk soon.

EUSTACE: What's your answer?

AGNES: They're coming.

ANNETTA: I'll think about it. I really will. Please go.
He'll suspect something if he even sees you in the hall.

EUSTACE: Okay…but only 'cause I don't want to get
you in no deep water. But think 'bout what I asked
you. I want a answer.

(EUSTACE *crosses right into* LIZZIE's *apartment.* AGNES
places iron door stop of apartment door. Closes door)

LIZZIE: *(From within)* Ow! You ain't had to push the
door so hard, boy. You should guess I was standin'
'hind it.

(EUSTACE *closes his door.)*

ANNETTA: *(She crosses left to cabinet, places bag on floor,
crosses up stage to stove, opens soup pot, turns burner.
Crosses to up center table puts cover on cookie box, crosses
right with box and home-bound book. Places book on trunk,
crosses stage left to cabinet, places cookie box up stage corner
of oak cabinet.)* 'C'mon and help me.

(AGNES *starts to study her stenography.)*

ANNETTA: At least you can set the table.

AGNES: We have time. *(She crosses down stage sits stage
right chair at table.)*

ANNETTA: *(She places groceries in cabinet. Takes milk bottle
out of bag crosses left center places bottle in icebox.)* But you
said.

AGNES: I lied!

ANNETTA: What?

AGNES: I lied! It was for your own good.

ANNETTA: For my own good…just when I had him
where I wanted him. *(She crosses up stage to cabinet.*

Picks up bag. Folds it crosses up stage places it in grey cabinet.)

AGNES: You may have had him right where you wanted him…but if Papa had come in and caught the two of you "there" together…you know he'd put the rope to your behind…and then mine…and I'm damned sick and tired of gettin' welts on mine just because I'm the oldest and am supposed to be able to counsel you.

ANNETTA: *(She crosses to oak cabinet opens drawer takes tablecloth.)* I was coming in.

AGNES: At your own convenience. You must be in love, because you ain't using your head. Well I ain't in love so I don't look forward to being flogged for that gorilla. He's not bad looking…for one of them…and, lord, is he big.

(ANNETTA crosses up center of table spreads tablecloth.)

ANNETTA: As big as a tree.

AGNES: I wasn't referring to just his height.

ANNETTA: I don't know what on earth you could possible mean, *(She crosses left to wall cabinet opens takes six bowls, crosses right to up stage table, places bowls.)* but as "de nigguhs" is wont to say, "thank de lawd for dem stove-pipe pants."

AGNES: "Amen." Well, at least he's interested in you, thanks be praised. The way you 've been mooning and whining whenever you see him, I couldn't have stood it much longer if he hadn't taken the bait. But, please be careful…whatever you do. Papa would kill you both…not to mention…ME.…

ANNETTA: Don't be silly, girl! He's bigger than Papa. *(She crosses sits chair at left of table.)* Besides, it's not going to get that serious. I won't let it. I'm just having a little fun…that's all.

AGNES: That had better be all 'cause Papa's all but got you wedded and bedded to Mr Wallace.

ANNETTA: If he thinks I'd even entertain thoughts of that man crossing me...he needs dusting...besides Mr Wallace is more your type,

(AGNES *stops correcting papers, places inside folder.*)

ANNETTA: you being so brainy and all. He's so crazy about Papa he ought to be nuts about you....

AGNES: Hah! The man I'm going to marry hasn't been born yet.... (*She stands, crosses left to oak cabinet. Places folder on up stage arch chair. Opens cabinet drawer takes six napkins.*)

ANNETTA: Don't worry... (*She stands, crosses up center table.*) One day your Prince Charming will come marching down 63rd Street wearing white knickers, checkered stockings and flapped oxfords and sweep you off your feet....

AGNES: As long as I land on my feet instead of my ass. (*She crosses right to* ANNETTA, *pushes left table chair under table.*) As you Cinderella, you just keep on dreaming about your giant-sized Prince Charming but right now if you don't finish setting the table...

(AGNES *tosses napkins on table.* ANNETTA *picks up napkins.*)

AGNES: ...even your fairy godmother won't be able to prevent Papa from breaking your glass slippers...not to mention your black behind....

(AGNES *exits left through arch, chased by* ANNETTA.)

(*A bit later, the table is set with soup plates.*)

(NIMROD *and* SOLOMON *enter hall from street carrying wooden tub with beef brine, crosses left to* BARTON *apartment door.*)

NIMROD: C'mon, man . Hold up your side....

(NIMROD *opens apartment door.* ANNETTA *crosses to hall table takes flowers.*) If this shit spills and stinks me up, I'm gonna...

SOLOMON: You ain't gonna do shit.

(NIMROD *and* SOLOMON *enter kitchen.*)

SOLOMON: Think 'cause you the oldest, you gonna kick my ass all the time and I'm supposed to just stand there and let you...?

NIMROD: As long as I'm the oldest...

(ANNETTA *crosses right to kitchen table.*)

AGNES: You two had better stop talking like street niggers and... (*She stands crosses to boys.*) ...what in the hell is that....

ANNETTA: (*She crosses up right to* NIMROD *and* SOLOMON.) Get it out of here!

SOLOMON: It's Papa's beef brine!

AGNES & ANNETTA: What?

SOLOMON: Beef brine.

(NIMROD *and* SOLOMON *crosses left, places tub in front of oak cabinet.*)

NIMROD: He has to soak his foot in it from now on... every night.

(SOLOMON *crosses right sits on trunk.*)

ANNETTA: (*She crosses, puts flowers in center of table, stands up center of table.*) The doctors said that...?

NIMROD: *He* said it. Mama told us this morning.

SOLOMON: And we have to get it from Mr Wallace's store everyday and bring it home....

AGNES: (*She crosses right to* NIMROD.) You brought that through the streets?

NIMROD: Where else? We can't fly...we're the Barton brothers...not the Wrights.

AGNES: As if we weren't laughed at enough.... *(She crosses right, places folder on trunk.)*

ANNETTA: As if the house didn't smell enough with that pipe of his....

AGNES: Now this....

SOLOMON: And don't forget, we ain't even took the cover off yet....

AGNES: "Haven't taken. Haven't yet taken off the cover! Can't you try to speak properly? Honestly, you two get more American every day.

(ANNETTA crosses right below oval table to stage right chair [FLORIE's chair] crosses up right center.)

NIMROD: We are Americans. We were born here, re member. You and Annetta is *(He stands does monkey imitation.)* the monkey chasers.

SOLOMON: *(He does monkey imitation.)* Monkey chasers! Coconut eaters! Sugar cane suckers!

AGNES: Doesn't matter where you're born...you're still West Indians.

(ANNETTA picks up, up right chair crosses to up center table places chair.)

AGNES: Try to escape if you want to but you'll never be common niggers.

ANNETTA: Oh...I wish all this talk about niggers and West Indians would stop. We're going to hear enough about it soon enough any way. It's bad enough he's coming home and those damned Sunday parades starting up again.

NIMROD: God damn....I forgot all about them.

AGNES: I didn't...I was thinking about conveniently losing my tin helmet...but I'd only have to get another.

NIMROD: Hey maybe with him limpin' and all now... maybe he can't march on Sundays no more.

AGNES: Nimrod...do you really believe that...? I mean do you really believe that...?

NIMROD: Suppose not...

SOLOMON: Well I like the parades.

(AGNES crosses to NIMROD.)

NIMROD: Well... Shit...you crazy.

(AGNES crosses to SOLOMON.)

SOLOMON: Aw...fuck you.

(AGNES crosses to NIMROD.)

NIMROD: Fuck you back in the same old crack.

ANNETTA: (She crosses left to cabinet, takes spoons from drawer, crosses right to table, places spoons on napkins.) "You're not negroes...you're not colored...you're edenites for you come from Eden...there would be no palefaced people had not an Edenite woman in her folly wished upon the pale moon.... Americans have allowed themselves to remain less than men...and nigger this and nigger that...." I just don't want to hear it...you understand? I'm just sick and tired of it all.

SOLOMON: What's wrong with her...?

(ANNETTA crosses right to NIMROD.)

AGNES: Annetta doesn't like to talk about niggers anymore 'cause she's got a case on one...next door.

NIMROD: No shit? Thought something was goin' on. Hey...come to think of it...I saw him in the hall before and he looked like he was drawing a picture of Annetta...tried to cover it so I couldn't see....

(In the hall LIZZIE enters hall from her apartment, sits in chair at window.)

ANNETTA: A picture of me?

NIMROD: I couldn't say for sure.... He tried to cover it up so fast....

SOLOMON: *(Putting on a West Indian accent and imitating his father.)* You mean, the girl has rose eyes for a south ape.

ANNETTA: *(She crosses left to table finishes placing napkins.)* Shut up!

NIMROD: *(Also imitation. He crosses up center to apartment door.)* "Not a bit of it! Not a bit of it! You hear. Not a bit of it! No slave's leavings will ever t'row down one of my pure British subject princesses and tup dey legs across dem." *(He crosses right center laughingly falls to floor.)*

SOLOMON: Who would dare? Not to my little lambs.... They've never been touched and never will be at least not by a slave. *(He lifts NIMROD.)* ...a dirty, jack-leg rogue American slave.

(FLORIE appears in hall top of steps; looks down steps.)

AGNES: Get up from there, sah!

(ANNETTA crosses to cabinet, takes glass, crosses up to brine, crosses down right center to NIMROD. NIMROD crosses down center, crosses left below table, ANNETTA follows with brine. AGNES crosses up center above table to left of table. NIMROD crosses up center. SOLOMON crosses up center to towel rack takes towel. AGNES pushes NIMROD to floor. ANNETTA kneels threatens to pour brine on NIMROD. SOLOMON hits AGNES with towel. AGNES fights him down stage right, crosses left to table, takes napkin defends self against SOLOMON crosses down right.)

AGNES: You but a ram-goat trying to make mannish water...and with a British subject? Not a bit of it!

(BARTON *enters hall, crosses left to apartment door.*)

LIZZIE: Hey, Florie.

FLORIE: Hello, Lizzie.

(*No acknowledgement from* BARTON.)

LIZZIE: I know you glad your man's home.... Bet be glad to be home too.

(FLORIE *nods.* BARTON *pushes open his door and discovers the kids chasing each other around the room....*MRS BARTON *enters behind him and closes the door.* SOLOMON *sees* BARTON *[soft voice "Papa's home"]* AGNES *stops hitting* SOLOMON *crosses above table, crosses left to* ANNETTA. ANNETTA *and* NIMROD *stand.* ANNETTA *crosses up right to* AGNES. *[*ANNETTA *stands down stage beef brine.]* LIZZIE *puts her ears to the door to hear what she can.*)

(BARTON *stands landing,* FLORIE *behind him.*)

BARTON: Bacchanals? Bacchanals in the home? Is it revelry you want? (*He crosses into kitchen.*) Well, I can arrange it before you go to bed this night. Behaving like jamettes!

FLORIE: (*She enters apartment crosses right to trunk places hat and pocketbook.*) Joseph...sit in your chair.... The walk upstairs must have exhausted you. Annetta bas prepared a homecoming dinner for you. The table is set. Come!

(FLORIE *leads* BARTON *to his chair.*)

FLORIE: The food is ready?

ANNETTA: Yes ma'am.

FLORIE: Gentlemen...please wash your hands....

NIMROD: We did already...

FLORIE: Then sit in your places...

(SOLOMON *shakes* BARTON's *hand crosses left below table, crosses up center, hangs dish towel, right sink rack, crosses to down stage arch chair, crosses right, place down stage right corner of table, crosses sits down left table chair.* AGNES *tries to pull out the chair for her father.*)

BARTON: I am not a cripple.

AGNES: Sorry Papa. I mean…it's good to have you home.

(NIMROD *crosses to up stage arch chair, crosses to table place down stage left corner of table.* AGNES *takes* BARTON's *hat and newspaper, crosses left through arch. Places paper on table, hat on coatrack.*)

(ANNETTA *crosses right to* BARTON, *kisses on cheek;* NIMROD *sits up left table chair.*)

ANNETTA: I made chicken-foot soup…Papa.…

BARTON: But naturally. (*He stands up center table.*) I am ready. You may begin .

(NIMROD *and* SOLOMON *stack bowls on table.* AGNES *crosses to table left of* BARTON. *Gets bowls and crosses to cabinet, places bowls.* ANNETTA *crosses to stove takes ladle uncovers soup.*)

FLORIE: Before we begin, Joseph… (*She crosses right closes apartment door; crosses down center to right of bar.*) the children and would like to say how thankful to God we are that you are home with us again.…

BARTON: AsIwas preparing to leave the hospital, a nurse told me that I should give thanks that I was going home in one piece. I believe she meant, as you probably do, Florie, that God was responsible for my recovery…and was therefore to be thanked. I told her that I do give thanks, but since I alone was responsible for my own recovery…the thanks was due to myself only! God, it would seem, has no time for the things I have to do. Eat!

(FLORIE *crosses down to down center table chair.*)

(ANNETTA *ladles soup into bowls.* AGNES *places them in front of* FLORIE *and the seated* BARTON *men. They sit and eat only after the rest of the family is served. Sound of* BARTON *slurping soup*)

(*Out—in black*)

(SOLOMON *places down right table chair at down right arch; crosses down left; gets lamp on bookcase; 2 books off trunk; crosses left sits stage right table chair.* NIMROD *places napkins and spoons on cabinet up left chair to up stage arch; crosses left sits stage left table.* AGNES *moves brine down stage front of cabinet; gets dish towel.* ANNETTA *takes 2 bowls, puts in sink drain, crosses to sink gets dish cloth.* FLORIE *crosses to right to trunk, takes hat and purse, exits thru hall.* BARTON *takes cane exits left thru arch.*)

(*Sometime after the meal.* BARTON *and* FLORIE *are in their respective rooms.* NIMROD *and* SOLOMON *are reading "home-bound" books.* AGNES *and* ANNETTA *are finishing the dishes.*)

(ANNETTA *places second bowl in drain.*)

AGNES: I'm glad that's the last of them. (*She takes bowl from drain dries with towel, places with other in cabinet.*) Can't think of anything I hate to do more than wipe dishes....

ANNETTA: (*She crosses down center table, takes down center chair* [FLORIE's] *and crosses right places between bookcase and trunk; crosses left to up center table takes up center* [BARTON's] *chair places up right center left of pipe stand table.*) Try washing them for a change...then maybe you'd appreciate just having to dry. (*She crosses up center table takes lamp and flowers in vase, crosses left places up stage arch chair.*) One of these days people're going to be looking for me to cook (*She crosses up center table takes tablecloth, crosses up stage to sink, shakes crumbs in sink.)* something or sew something or dust something and I'm going to be gone…just not here.

AGNES: Well…

(AGNES crosses to ANNETTA, they fold tablecloth.)

AGNES: …if you think just because I will be the only daughter around here to take your place in the kitchen, Cinderella, then you have another think coming!

NIMROD: What you two whisperin' 'bout?

ANNETTA: Both of you'd better keep on studying. *(She crosses to up stage arch chair takes lamp, crosses right, places center table; crosses left to up stage arch chair takes vase, crosses into hall places on table.)* You know he's going to ask you questions.

AGNES: *(She places tablecloth in cabinet drawer.)* It wouldn't have hurt if you had read a little each night. You wouldn't have been so far behlnd now…

(ANNETTA crosses up center to sink gets dish cloth crosses left center wipes icebox.)

AGNES: …and risk getting your behinds whipped.

NIMROD: I don't see why we gotta study these dumb old books. I don't see why I gotta study no African history…I ain't African.

AGNES: *(She puts napkins in drawer.)* You're no European either and you're learning European history in school.

NIMROD: *(He stands, crosses left down stage of brine.)* You so fuckin' smart.

AGNES: What'd you say? Boy, I'm gonna get you.

(AGNES kicks brine [top falls off]. SOLOMON stands, crosses up left of table. She tries to kick at him but kicks the tub of beef brine…spilling some…. She screams.)

NIMROD & SOLOMON: Ooooooh!

BARTON: *(From within)* What are you about out there?

NIMROD: Agnes kicked over your beef brine. *(He crosses right side stage left table.)*

SOLOMON: It's all over the floor Papa. *(He crosses right sits right table chair.)*

ANNETTA: *(She crosses into arch way.)* It was an accident, Papa. Nimrod and Solomon didn't push it all the way to the wall and Agnes...didn't see it. *They* didn't push it back far enough, only a little spilled.

AGNES: *(She sits up stage arch chair.)* I wish it had all spilled!

ANNETTA: *(She crosses to sink.)* Me, too.

BARTON: I'll be out just now.

FLORIE: *(She enters from up stage room with sewing basket.)* There's not much wasted, Joseph. Just a bit. *(She crosses to up right corner of table, places basket on table.)* Annetta, clean it up...quickly.

ANNETTA: *(She crosses to grey cabinet takes rags, crosses to brine wipes it up.)* Mama, it smells so bad.

FLORIE: Hush, girl...

AGNES: I hope I didn't break my toe. It sure hurts.

FLORIE: Before you go to bed, soak your foot in hot water and epsom salts.

SOLOMON: Why don't you use the beef brine...?

FLORIE: *(Laughing)* Hush boy.

ANNETTA: It does stink, Mama.

FLORIE: I know, girl. I know.

(BARTON, *entering in robe and nightclothes. He enters from down stage room, takes paper from table crosses right into kitchen.* FLORIE *crosses right sits chair right of trunk.*

BARTON *crosses right to* BARTON *chair, places right center spike marks.)*

BARTON: Nimrod, place that brine before my chair.

NIMROD: Yes, sir, *(He stands crosses to ottoman places left of trunk.)* c'mon, Solomon, help me.

(NIMROD crosses left to beef brine. SOLOMON stands.)

BARTON: I take it, you're not man enough to handle it alone?

NIMROD: Yes, sir.

(SOLOMON, sits. NIMROD takes brine cover off crosses up center places right of sink, crosses to brine, takes brine, crosses right places front of BARTON's chair.)

NIMROD: Never mind, Solomon.

BARTON: All right now! *(He sits.)* Now then…the four of you…in your places.

(AGNES, ANNETTA, NIMROD, SOLOMON, line up diagonally from door, facing BARTON.)

BARTON: Mistress Agnes…

(AGNES steps to BARTON.)

BARTON: …what about the typing?

AGNES: I'm not taking it anymore.

BARTON: What's this?

AGNES: I mean…my instructress says there's no more she can teach me. She says I'm just too fast so I'm just helping her instruct the other students.… She says I'm ready for work.

BARTON: It would seem she says a great many things but I will come to the school and say to her that you will no longer assist her unless you receive remuneration for your services. The shorthand?

AGNES: Same thing.… My speed only increases. She says I…if I was allowed to work you wouldn't have to spend your money on summer school.…

BARTON: I will be the judge of when you're ready for employment. The piano?

AGNES: Mr Lewis says I should be preparing for a concert. If not…I shouldn't take lessons anymore.

BARTON: You have a lesson tomorrow evening, correct?

AGNES: Yes, sir.

BARTON: I will go there with you and inform Mr Lewis that he is paid to teach you how to play the piano…and not for advice on how I invest my money.

FLORIE: You shouldn't go out so soon, Joseph.

BARTON: Nonsense!

(AGNES *crosses sits up stage arch chair.*)

BARTON: Annetta…

(ANNETTA *crosses up left of table.*)

BARTON: I see you've not been wasting your time.… The house looks as clean as it always does. You manage well on the budget.

ANNETTA: Well I've found a store where food doesn't cost as much.

BARTON: Ah, yes. That would explain why Mr Wallace told me he had not seen much of you.…

ANNETTA: The new store…it saves money.

BARTON: It would seem that my family doesn't think me a good provider.… They worry so about my ability with money. I would like some cocoa…if there is some.…

ANNETTA: There's just enough.…

BARTON: Then you will go to Mr Wallace's and purchase more. And don't bring American cocoa into my house because it costs less. Is there enough for your mother to have a cup?

ANNETTA: Yes sir.

(ANNETTA *crosses to center to icebox, gets milk crosses to stove.* AGNES *stands, takes four cups from cabinet.* ANNETTA *pours milk into saucepan,* AGNES *opens cocoa, places cubes in milk.*)

NIMROD: Can I have some too, Papa.

SOLOMON: Me, too....

AGNES: I thought you always said that home cocoa was too greasy for you.

NIMROD: *(He crosses to* AGNES.*)* I ain't said I ain't liked it.... I mean... *(He steps to* BARTON.*)*

BARTON: What language is this you are speaking, young sir? Is it supposed to be English? Well, Florie, it appears that while I have been hospitalized...and you have been at your jobs...our young men have been taking the first steps to becoming...Americans.

SOLOMON: Not I Papa.

(NIMROD *glares at* SOLOMON.*)*

FLORIE: Joseph, they play with the other boys in the street. It's natural for them to pick up some of their...

BARTON: But they shan't bring what they pick up into my house. If this is an example of what's to come, then I shall have to put an end to their consorting in the streets with...

NIMROD: I'm sorry, Papa.

BARTON: I gave you leave to interrupt me with apologies?

NIMROD: I'm sorry, Papa.

BARTON: Let us see where else you've fallen down. Before I went to the hospital, I believe we were discussing Hannibal. In my absence, I presume you've continued with your reading. Tell me now, if you will, what was the name of his father?

NIMROD: *(He steps to* BARTON *up right table chair.)* Whose father?

SOLOMON: Hannibal's

*(*EUSTACE *enters top step hall, crosses to* LIZZIE's *door.)*

*(*ANNETTA *and* AGNES *are behind* BARTON *trying to mouth the answer to* NIMROD *.* EUSTACE *comes up the stairs… sketch pad in hand…as he goes toward his door he flips through the page….)*

BARTON: I'm waiting.

*(*EUSTACE *suddenly turns…goes to the* BARTON's *door and knocks.)*

NIMROD: There's someone knocking at… *(He crosses to landing.)*

BARTON: You think me hard of hearing?

NIMROD: No, sir. *(He crosses up right of table.)*

BARTON: What I didn't hear was your answer.

*(*EUSTACE *knocks again.)*

FLORIE: I will see who it is. *(She puts sewing down crosses up stage to door.)*

BARTON: Why do you not admit it if you don't know. Trying to bluff me is tantamount to telling me a lie. You could have saved yourself what's to come by not taking me for an ass.…

(Another knock. FLORIE *opens the door.)*

FLORIE: Oh ?

EUSTACE: Evenin, ma'am.

FLORIE: Is there something wrong with your aunt?

EUSTACE: No, ma'am. If you don't mind, I'd like to talk with you…

FLORIE: Me?

EUSTACE: That is, I'd like to speak with your husband.

FLORIE: My husband?

BARTON: Who is this?

(FLORIE *closes door, leaves it slightly ajar.*)

FLORIE: It's Mrs Harris' nephew…from next door.   .

EUSTACE: (*He sticks head in door.*) My name is Eustace Baylor, sir. I'd much like to speak with…

(NIMROD *crosses left stands down stage arch,* SOLOMON *crosses sits up stage arch chair.*)

BARTON: Show the young fellow in…Florie.

FLORIE: Come in…Eustace.

EUSTACE: (*He crosses into* BARTON *apartment.*) Thank you, ma'am.

(ANNETTA *crosses left to arch.*)

BARTON: And where are you going, Annetta.

ANNETTA: I felt a little tired. I was going to lie down.

BARTON: Sudden, isn't it? Well…if you don't feel too tired…I would appreciate it if you watched the cocoa… suppose it boiled over.…

(ANNETTA *crosses to stove stirs cocoa.*)

BARTON: You must excuse me, Mr Baylor…is it? My sons are in the midst of their evening lessons.…

EUSTACE: Evening lessons?

BARTON: It's the summer season, I know but that's no reason for education to be neglected. Much that young men should know is not taught in the schools.

It therefore behooves us...the parents...to make up
the gaps with knowledge to which the teachers are not
privy, would you not agree?

EUSTACE: Well...I can't say that I see the hook in'
'tween education and the toilet but...

BARTON: You see, I have tried to instill it into my
children that knowledge is power. I want my children
to know that those in power in this country respect
knowledge as a great equalizer, having that kind of
power gives your enemies a certain kind of fear....
Would you agree to that?

EUSTACE: Where I come from...if those kind of folks are
scared of you...they just hang you...

(ANNETTA *pours cocoa in cup crosses right to right of*
BARTON.)

BARTON: But wouldn't knowledge allow one to avoid
your enemies...?

ANNETTA: The cocoa's ready, Papa.

(AGNES *pours cocoa into two cups passes one to* SOLOMON.)

FLORIE: Would you care for some cocoa...Eustace?

EUSTACE: No, thank you ma'am. I just et.

BARTON: I don't think he's come for a social visit,
Florie. Sit down here where I can see you...young
fellow.

(EUSTACE *crosses right, sits* FLORIE *chair.*)

EUSTACE: Thank you.

(FLORIE *crosses right up stage of* BARTON *to trunk, takes
sewing basket.*)

BARTON: Agnes.

(AGNES *crosses right to* BARTON.)

BARTON: Go with Nimrod and Solomon to my room and see that they get deeply into those books.

(NIMROD *and* SOLOMON *cross right to table take books, cross left through arch exits down stage room.* AGNES *follows boys exit.* ANNETTA *follows* AGNES.)

BARTON: No, Annetta. You will stay!

(ANNETTA *stops crosses right stand up right of table.*)

BARTON: Now, what can do for you?

EUSTACE: Heard 'bout your accident. See you soakin' your foot in beef brine.

FLORIE: (*She crosses left sits chair left of table with sewing basket.*) You're familiar with it?

EUSTACE: Don't smell too good but it come in handy every once in a while. Back home we use it for all sorts of ailments.

(FLORIE *sits.*)

BARTON: Who is "we"?

EUSTACE: Us homeys from down the way...probably just something we all know about.

BARTON: Am I to believe you've come to my home to speak of cure-alls...?

EUSTACE: No, sir. Well...I'm a man who don't like to beat 'round the bush. Like to get right down to brass tacks as they say....

BARTON: Young fellow, you've come to speak with me about my daughter here. Is this not so?

EUSTACE: How'd you know?

BARTON: I was only hospitalized, sir.... Not unable to keep track of the welfare of my family.

EUSTACE: Well... *(He stands.)* ...long as the cat's out the bag. I'd like your permission to call on mistress 'Netta here.

BARTON: Why?

EUSTACE: Hunh?

BARTON: I asked why?

ANNETTA: Papa, may I please go to my room?

BARTON: No!

EUSTACE: I'm sorry, 'Netta. I didn't want to cause you no embarrassment...

BARTON: Annetta...if you're looking for an excuse to go to your room...you 'll soon have it.

(FLORIE goes to ANNETTA.)

BARTON: Now...I believe I asked you a question, sir. Why do you want to call on my daughter?

EUSTACE: 'Cause she...well...I hadn't thought... *(He sits.)* but I guess she's the only person I ever seen who hold herself like she do. High ! You know? Don't get me wrong. Both your girls is ladies but there's just something 'bout mistress 'Netta that takes me...just takes me. First day I got here and saw her comin' down the street...well...ain't got no fancy words to tell what I was feelin'. Even forgot to tip my cap 'till she had already passed. I remember thinkin' that she won't think I got no manners...I was just starin' so. Durn near...'scuse me...pretty near jump for joy when I find out she livin' cross the hall from me....

BARTON: And you were able to recognize that she was a lady of some quality.

EUSTACE: More than that...

BARTON: What could be more than a lady...? A queen perhaps...?

EUSTACE: Don't know nothin' 'bout no queens.

BARTON: But you do know ladies.

EUSTACE: My mother was one.

BARTON: No doubt.

EUSTACE: She's a star! ...That's what she is.

BARTON: Aha! A star...

EUSTACE: She shines...for me.

BARTON: And what is a star? Something that burns the hands of those foolhardy enough to reach for it with the naked hand. "Reach" ...because it is not easily available to you.... So you want to reach upward for the stars and drag one down. Drag it to earth with you and your kind....

EUSTACE: My kind? What do you mean my kind? ... You mean...'cause I'm from south? Man, you crazy. This ain't even your country.... It's mine and you can't talk to me like...

BARTON: Really? This is your country? Go out and prove it. You live where you're told. You do as you're told. They call you "negro". Were this really, truly your country, would it not be called "negro land"?

EUSTACE: Well, shit. *(He stands.)* If you ain't satisfied here why the fuck don't you go back to where the fuck you come from?

FLORIE: *(She stands, crosses right to* ANNETTA.*)* Joseph... for God's sake... Allow Annetta to go to her room. She cannot hear language like this.

*(*ANNETTA *and* FLORIE *cross left thru arch exit up stage room.)*

FLORIE: Come, Annetta.

ANNETTA: *(Crying)* Oh, Mama.

EUSTACE: *(He crosses left to arch.)* You gotta forgive me. It slipped out. He riled me.

FLORIE: Come girl.

BARTON: I would like you to know that I don't go back from whence I came because I think it more important to go from whence I was taken... You will pardon me if I don't get up...good evening sir.

EUSTACE: *(He crosses down left of table.)* That's it? ...You think it's gonna end here?

BARTON: It's best...any chance you might have had...

EUSTACE: Aw, shit man. *(He crosses right down of table.)* I ain't never had no chance with you and you know it full well. Don't even know what made me knock on your door. I came back to pick up my sandwiches I forgot to take to the pool room....

BARTON: I'm told you spend your nights in a "pool room".

EUSTACE: I work there. My aunt owns it and I work there. Didn't your tattle-tale tell you that, too? *(He crosses right to* FLORIE's *chair takes pad and cap, crosses left to up right of table.)* 'Stead of comin' here, I shoulda. followed my mind 'stead o' whatever the fuck I was following. But, no. I had to come here... *(He takes out sketch of* ANNETTA *places on table.)* Even brought this picture I drew of 'Netta. Thought I'd surprise you...she ain't even know nothin' 'bout it. Figured I could show you I was somethin' more than another nigger off the corner. But you ain't nothin' but a crazy bastard... tellin' people...tellin' colored people they ain't good enough for you. You think you white. That's what's wrong with you...you think you white.

BARTON: To the contrary...I know that I am black...I am black therefore I must be even more selective in

how I maintain it's purity.... I cannot allow pollution.
Now leave...

EUSTACE: It ain't gona end here.

BARTON: Mark me well. Come near my daughter and I
will kill you.

EUSTACE: So you think I'm worth killing, monkey
chaser?

BARTON: You're worth nothing, ape. But my blood is
worth keeping pure.

(BARTON *and* EUSTACE *look at each other.)*

EUSTACE: *(Muttering as he goes)* Ol' fool, that beef brine
don't cure shit. *(He exits thru apartment door, crosses right
enters* LIZZIE's *apartment.)*

FLORIE: *(She enters from up stage room, through arch,
crosses right to left of* BARTON.*)* He's gone?

BARTON: *(He begins to dry his foot.)* For now.... Why did
you not tell me what was going on?

FLORIE: What was going on, Joseph ? Annetta tells me
all they've ever done is say hello to each other... *(She
crosses to smoke stand right of* BARTON *takes cocoa.)*

BARTON: I had to hear it from others.

FLORIE: From whom? Mr Wallace? *(She crosses left above*
BARTON, *up center to stove, pours cocoa in saucepan.)* Since
he plans on Annetta for himself, I am not surprised.

BARTON: And what's wrong with his intentions? He
has property. He believes in the things I believe in...
and... *(He puts house shoes on.)* most important...he's
one of us.

(FLORIE *crosses up center to sink, puts cup and spoon in
sink.)*

FLORIE: *(She crosses to left of* BARTON.*)* So all he could do
while you were lying in the hospital was to run and fill

you with suspicion. Well, he seems to have had more time for visiting than I did Joseph, I hold down three jobs a week. Everyday I come home from the laundry and I can hardly keep my eyes open. On Thursday the Jew gives me enough ironing to keep me busy for an entire week. Then the other woman tries to kill me with her work. How can I see if anything is going on when Ican hardly see to walk home? You want me to tell you suspicions too?

BARTON: Call Annetta.

FLORIE: *(She crosses right, above* BARTON, *sits chair right of trunk.)* I won't be a party to this...Joseph. The girl has done nothing.

BARTON: Annetta!

*(*ANNETTA *opens door up stage room.* NIMROD *enters from down stage room crosses right to up stage arch.* AGNES, NIMROD *and* SOLOMON *come out.)*

BARTON: I called you?

*(*SOLOMON *and* NIMROD *retreat.* AGNES *enters from down stage room crosses right to left center, left of table.)*

AGNES: Papa, please. Annetta didn't do anything. Every time he said so much as a "hello", I was with her. Nothing ever happened.

BARTON: You were in on the conspiracy, also?

*(*AGNES *crosses left to down stage arch.)*

BARTON: Annetta don't let me call you again.

*(*ANNETTA *crosses thru arch, crosses right to up right of table wiping her eyes.)*

BARTON: I am ashamed of you.

ANNETTA: Yes, Papa.

BARTON: I expected more...and better from you who of all my children most resemble my own mother.

Time and again I have told you…if you hold yourself
like these people, you will be regarded as they are
regarded. Why would a daughter of mine encourage a
person such as that? He'll bring you down. What have
you to say for yourself?

ANNETTA: He didn't do anything…neither one of us
did anything.

BARTON: Then what would lead him to believe he had
the right to barge in here and declare himself….

ANNETTA: All right…Papa…it probably was my fault.
I spoke to him a few times. He asked me…he…he just
asked me if I would go some place with him.

BARTON: Some place like where…?

ANNETTA: He just meant the moving pictures…and
places like that…like the band concerts in the park…
block parties…places like that…and told him I would
think about it.

BARTON: You would think about it?

ANNETTA: I just wanted something to think about.
Something I could decide for myself…and I was only
entertaining the thought because it was fun….

BARTON: Fun?

ANNETTA: Look, Papa, I don't do anything except cook
and clean and wash…and I don't really mind 'cause I
know things aren't that easy with us and I don't mind
that it's Agnes who gets all the chances at other things
because she's the oldest and she bas all the brains…
and deserves the chance to become a good secretary or
something. I know Mama has to work and someone's
got to do things in the house, and I don't even mind
Nimrod and Solomon being treated like kings just
because they're boys…. But Papa…you come home
from the hospital and all you tell me is that I kept the

house clean.... You can't blame me for wanting to be
something other than a drudge.

BARTON: *(He stands crosses around his chair to right of*
ANNETTA.*)* What has all this to do with your parading
yourself before something unworthy of you...?

ANNETTA: Don't you see Papa...someone is interested
in me...just me. Someone cares about how I feel.
Papa...it's summertime...and I'm eighteen.

BARTON: Apparently an eighteen year old fool....

ANNETTA: I only know that someone care enough
about me to walk in here even though he knows how
you feel and declares himself to your face. And I love
him for it.

(BARTON slaps ANNETTA.)

FLORIE: Girl you don't know what you're saying!

AGNES: *(She crosses to left center, left of table.)* Annetta!

ANNETTA: *(Awed at her own news.)* That's right...! I do
love him. He came over.

BARTON: *(He goes to his room and opens the door. He*
crosses left to wall cupboard gets rope from hook. To
NIMROD *and* SOLOMON*)* Come out of there and go to
your mother's room.

*(*NIMROD *and* SOLOMON *enter from down stage room, stand*
under arch.)

ANNETTA: *(She crosses right, above BARTON chair to*
FLORIE.*)* He came over.

FLORIE: *(She crosses left, passing ANNETTA above BARTON*
chair to right of BARTON.) Joseph...you can't.

BARTON: Does my wife now defy me in my own house?

FLORIE: Will you beat me, too?

(BARTON crosses right to beef brine, places rope in brine,
ANNETTA *backs down stage right, below oval table.)*

FLORIE: She's a young woman. You can't beat her as if she were a child.

BARTON: *(Pointing* ANNETTA *to his room.)* She has the irresponsible mouth of a child. The irrational brain of a child. Maturity has to be beaten into her.

AGNES: Papa...she didn't know what she was saying. She didn't mean it.

NIMROD: Papa...please don't.

*(*ANNETTA *crosses left dinner table, left center to arch;* SOLOMON *crosses to* ANNETTA, *grabbing* ANNETTA *and crying.)*

SOLOMON: Annetta! Annetta!

ANNETTA: Don't cry, Solomon.

BARTON: You want something to cry for, young man?

*(*NIMROD *pulls* SOLOMON *away. Both of them go crying, into their mother's room.* ANNETTA *walks toward* BARTON's *room, undressing as she goes.* BARTON *follows her into his room, closes the door. Silence! Then the sound of rope whirring through the air...striking flesh, immediately followed by an ear-piercing scream.)*

AGNES: I wish he had died! I do! I wish that damned streetcar had killed him. I wish it had cut his legs off. I wish...

*(*AGNES *is interrupted by a sharp slap from* FLORIE, *who promptly embraces her. The two of them crying,* FLORIE *inaudibly.* NIMROD *and* SOLOMON *are at the open door of their mother's room, holding each other and crying all the while, more sounds of rope splitting the air and biting into flesh...and more screams.* LIZZIE *has come out of her apartment and is listening at the* BARTON's *door. Suddenly, silence! The boys close the door of their mother's room.* BARTON *comes out, the now blood-reddened rope in his hand and looking neither left nor right, sits in his chair.* FLORIE

and AGNES *run to* ANNETTA *in the room.* BARTON *lights
his pipe as* FLORIE *runs into the toilet. She comes out with a
dampened towel.)*

FLORIE: *(She crosses up right edge table.)* I know why
you did this. Mark me well, one of these days one of
our children will kill you...in some way, one of them
will kill you...and so help me Christ...I'll stand beside
them before the world. I, alone, know why you did
this. *(She crosses left, exit* BARTON *bedroom.)*

(Lights come down on scene. BARTON, *puffing on his pipe
and* LIZZIE *walking slowly back to her apartment, and*
BARTON *ripping up the drawing of* ANNETTA *that* EUSTACE
has left...)

(Out)

END OF ACT ONE

ACT TWO

(*Some days later.* SOLOMON *sitting stage left table eating oatmeal.* NIMROD *sitting stage right table eating oatmeal.* ANNETTA *standing at* BARTON *chair, shakes shirt.*)

(AGNES *enters from up stage room with folder crosses right to* ANNETTA.)

ANNETTA: But you don't have to.

AGNES: Yes, I do. I've let you wash that whole load of clothes...and I shouldn't have...'though, Lord knows, I never could get things as clean as you...

SOLOMON: You for sure ain't no housekeeper, that's for sure.

AGNES: (*She crosses to center table props basket against table.*) But I'm going to hang them to dry...and that's that. You just come along and sit.

(ANNETTA *sits* BARTON *chair.*)

AGNES: Let the sun get to that back.

FLORIE: (*She enters from up stage room with shopping bag, uniform in bag, crosses up left center to stove. Looks in soup pot. Places bag and pocket book up stage arch chair.*) I'm ready to go now. Remember...you are not to eat any of the soup before your father comes in from the clinic. Agnes, today is my day at Mrs Grossman's. Meet me at the back of her house promptly at three.

AGNES: Yes ma'am.

FLORIE: *(She crosses right to left of* ANNETTA.*)* Annetta… are you feeling okay?

ANNETTA: I'm feeling all right…Mama. *(She crosses up to left of* FLORIE.*)*

FLORIE: Well…don't do too much. You shouldn't have washed these things…

ANNETTA: I wanted something to do, Mama. I couldn't stay in that room…looking at the walls any longer… besides…I just feel better being up.

FLORIE: *(She crosses down to* NIMROD, *kisses him on cheek.)* Nimrod, when you and Solomon get through with your porridge, you wash your bowls and you can go over to Mrs Cammey's and play with Raymond…but mind you…be here when your father comes in…about three… *(She crosses left to up stage arch chair, turns crosses to* SOLOMON *kisses him on cheek, crosses to up stage arch chair takes bag and pocket book.)* …all right? I'm off.

*(*FLORIE *crosses right to apartment door exit to hall.* AGNES *puts basket on floor.)*

FLORIE: Annetta…be careful, please.

*(*AGNES *crosses right to door.)*

ANNETTA: I know Mama.

FLORIE: Good bye. *(She exits down steps.)*

AGNES: Okay, Nimrod… *(She crosses to apartment closes door, crosses left to up stage arch chair, gets folder crosses right to door.)* …hand me the basket. Solomon open the door…come on Annetta.

ANNETTA: Ready.

*(*ANNETTA *stands, crosses to door;* SOLOMON *stands, crosses right to door opens.* NIMROD *stands takes two bowls crosses up center, places scrub board right of sink, places bowls in sink. Crosses right to basket picks it up.)*

(ANNETTA *crosses into hall.*)

AGNES: Oh, damn.

ANNETTA: What?

AGNES: Can't very well hang up clothes without clothes-pins. You go ahead...I'll get'em.

(AGNES *closes door.* ANNETTA *crosses to hall window looks out, crosses to* LIZZIE's *door listens, peaks through keyhole.* ANNETTA *goes to the roof.* AGNES *puts wash down in the hall and goes into the house.*)

AGNES: Okay...you can go ahead, now and remember afterward...the two of you stay on that fire escape and keep *your* eye a-cock.

NIMROD: Never mind that...you just drive it into Annetta's head that all four of us can get our ass kicked....

AGNES: Both of you stay on the fire escape and if one of you has to go pee or something, make sure one of you stays out there....

NIMROD: Stop givin' orders and go....

AGNES: Just remember....

SOLOMON: Okay, Okay.

(SOLOMON *opens door.* AGNES *goes.*)

NIMROD: *(Following her)* Agnes...

AGNES: What? *(She stops.)*

NIMROD: Don't you think you oughta take the clothes-pins with you?

AGNES: Smartie!

(AGNES *crosses left to clothes-pin basket up stage of icebox, crosses right exits into hall.* NIMROD *exits to hall with clothes basket.* SOLOMON *stands in doorway.* AGNES *puts folder and clothes-pin basket in clothes basket, takes basket from* NIMROD *exits up stairs to roof.)*

*(*NIMROD *crosses right, knocks on* LIZZIE'*s door. From within.)*

LIZZIE: Who is it…and so early.

NIMROD: Next door, Miss Lizzie. Nimrod Barton.

LIZZIE: Just a minute. *(Opens door)* What's wrong?

NIMROD: Noth in' ma'am. *(He crosses left to* SOLOMON.*)* Go'n on the fire 'scape, nigger.

*(*SOLOMON *crosses left exits down stage room.)*

LIZZIE: What you want?

NIMROD: I gotta talk with Eustace.

LIZZIE: 'Bout what?

NIMROD: I gotta talk with him. It's import.ant.

LIZZIE: Where your daddy?

NIMROD: At the clinic. Ma'am I gotta talk with Eustace.

EUSTACE: *(From within)* Who is it, Aunt Lizzie?

LIZZIE: Nobody! *(She pulls door close.)* Go 'way. Eustace ain't gettin' into no trouble with y'all Bartons.

NIMROD: *(Pushing past her and yelling inside.)* Eustace… it's me. Nimrod Barton.

*(*LIZZIE *grabs* NIMROD'*s collar pulls him back into hall.)*

LIZZIE: You fresh, boy. Goin' over me.

NIMROD: Don't mean to be but like I said…it's important.

EUSTACE: *(He enters crosses into hall.)* Okay…Aunt Lizzie. I'll take care of it.

LIZZIE: No! No! Can't you see trouble comin'? All the time I been livin' here I been to myself…'specially since Anse pass on. I ain't bad no trouble with nobody.

(ANNETTA *enters onto roof.)*

EUSTACE: And you ain't gonna have none now.

LIZZIE: But you gonna…and if you gonna…I'm gonna 'cause we kin boy. Your trouble is my trouble. And we don't have to look for none.…

EUSTACE: Don't fret yourself, now. I want you to go'n inside.

LIZZIE: I ain't *(She crosses right of* EUSTACE.*)* Whatever's got to be said…gotta be said in front of me. *(To* NIMROD*)* Now, what you here to say, boy?

*(*AGNES *enters onto roof crosses to clothesline starts to hang shirts.* ANNETTA *sits on stool stage right roof.)*

NIMROD: Well…

EUSTACE: It's okay.

*(*NIMROD *crosses down stage bringing* EUSTACE.*)*

NIMROD: My sister's on the roof.

EUSTACE: Yeah ? She say she wanna see me?

NIMROD: You oughta go up.

EUSTACE: She say she wanna see me?

NIMROD: You go'n up. My other sister's with her. My brother and me's gonna be on the fire 'scape watchin'. We'll let you know when…you know…I gotta go. *(He crosses left to* BARTON *door.)*

EUSTACE: Hey.

NIMROD: Hunh?

EUSTACE: Thanks.

NIMROD: Y'all be careful.… It's my ass, if you ain't. 'Scuse me ma'am. *(He enters* BARTON *apartment, closes door, crosses left exits down stage room.)*

*(*EUSTACE *crosses up left to steps to roof.)*

LIZZIE: You goin', hunh ?

EUSTACE: My future waitin' up there for me.

LIZZIE: So you ain't gon' pay me no rabbit-ass mind, hunh? Well, I'm gonna keep watch too. And when you hear me callin', don't you be lally-gaggin'. Bring it on down here, hear?

EUSTACE: I hear you.... *(He exits up stage.)*

ANNETTA: Spread 'em out more. There aren't that many things that you have to bunch 'em up.

AGNES: Okay! Okay!

ANNETTA: Well...it was your idea to do this...how do you expect to become a proper scullery maid if you can't hang clothes properly...?

AGNES: How...indeed .

(EUSTACE enters crosses center.)

EUSTACE: Hello!

AGNES: Hello!

ANNETTA: Agnes?

AGNES: It's okay. The boys are on the fire 'scape keeping a lookout.

EUSTACE: So's my aunt.

AGNES: Now, *(She crosses up stage around* EUSTACE *crosses between them.)* Mr Eustace Baylor. News has a habit of traveling around San Juan Hill faster than the natives can drum beat it out. No doubt, you know my sister went through close hell because of your bit of irresponsibility.

EUSTACE: Irresponsibility?

AGNES: You shouldn't have come over.

ANNETTA: Agnes!

AGNES: He shouldn't 've. Now let me finish. Annetta still seems to think you're worth going through what she went through...well I don't. But...that's you and her! I personally don't think any amount of whatever you all call it is worth all that pain. If the two of you get caught doing anything together, Annette's in deep trouble again. But that's not all. This time I'll probably get the same thing...probably worse.

EUSTACE: You?

AGNES: Yes...you can't possibly understand my father...but that's his way.

EUSTACE: Well why you gettin' in it?

AGNES: 'Cause she's in it. She's my sister. My father does preach our responsibility to each other. At any rate, Annetta's not thinking very clearly right now so someone has to...and that's me. I sure hope you're worth her getting her ass whipped cause you sure wouldn't be worth mine.

EUSTACE: Both you and your daddy some crazy 'bout me, ain't you?

AGNES: And for God's sake...please...be careful, if Nim and Solomon call you and tell you to come down...you go....
(EUSTACE *goes into a fit of laughter.*)

AGNES: What's so funny?

EUSTACE: My aunt just told, me the same thing.

AGNES: Nobody's said she didn't have sense. Well I have to (*She picks up folder.*) go to my class.... Now, you two talk, hear? Just talk. Please don't...just talk...eh? (*She exits up left roof door enters hall from roof and down steps to street.*)

EUSTACE: How you feel?

(ANNETTA *shrugs her shoulders.*)

ANNETTA: She didn't finish hanging these things. *(She stands crosses to basket.)*

EUSTACE: *(He picks up basket.)* Lemme do...it.

ANNETTA: No...I can do it. A man isn't supposed to do...stuff like that.

EUSTACE: No?

ANNETTA: No!

EUSTACE: What they supposed to do?

ANNETTA: I don't know.... Manly things, I guess.

EUSTACE: Like whip up on a girl...?

ANNETTA: I don't want to talk about that because you'll think it was your fault...and you'll feel you owe me something.... *(She puts basket down.)*

EUSTACE: We gonna have to talk 'bout it 'cause it was too my fault. I been lyin' 'wake nights...wonderin' what made me knock on your door. I still don't know.... I just had to, that's all. I'm sorry you went through that. It was too my fault.

ANNETTA: Try thinking of it in another way....

EUSTACE: Don't see how I can....

ANNETTA: Can't you think of it...as my having gone through it for you....

EUSTACE: That's nice...real nice.

ANNETTA: Forget it happened.... I don't want you to think about it anymore.... I really don't...just forget it happened, can you ?

EUSTACE: Can you? We startin' out on somethin' so we may's well get the ratty things cut loose...start clean.

(EUSTACE *puts his hand on* ANNETTA's *back, she winces.*)

ANNETTA: Oh... *(She pulls away.)*

EUSTACE: What's the matter ?

ANNETTA: *(Coyly)* Nothing. My back's not quite healed....

EUSTACE: Let me see.

ANNETTA: No....

EUSTACE: Let me see, 'Netta. *(He turns her around and pulls up her blouse.)* God damn ! What am I? Why somebody hate me so much...they do this to their own? ...What's so bad 'bout me?

ANNETTA: *(She crosses down right.)* You think he did this because he hates you...?

EUSTACE: You think it's 'cause he loves you?

ANNETTA: Yes...sort of...I understand him.

EUSTACE: Bless you then 'cause I think he's the closest thing I seen to the devil this side of hell....

ANNETTA: Eustace...he does love me. He wants what's best for me....

EUSTACE: And for him....

ANNETTA: Yes...and for him! I'm not saying he's right about it, but he thinks he knows what's best for me... and doing what he thinks best for me gives him his kind of happiness. I would like to say the same thing about you...Eustace. Don't you want to do what you think is best for me...?.

EUSTACE: Only I ain't gonna ever hurt you...that's the difference 'tween him and me...I hope God lay me under wherever I'm standin' if I would ever raise my hand to you....

ANNETTA: Well we don't have to talk about that because I'll never give you cause....

EUSTACE: Does that mean...you know...what we talked 'bout the other day...you going with me?

ANNETTA: Yes....

EUSTACE: I ain't gonna press you none 'bout it. I know your father don't like us niggers but...

ANNETTA: Didn't you hear me...I said, "yes".

EUSTACE: What...?

ANNETTA: If I didn't want to...do you think I'd have taken that...? Well, I just wouldn't have gone through it...that's all. You still want to, don't you?

EUSTACE: Still want to? Still want to? Man, oh man, oh man! Hey 63rd Street, look what I got.

(LIZZIE *stands crosses left to roof steps.*)

ANNETTA: Eustace, you're crazy.

EUSTACE: You got me, girl. You got me for life.

ANNETTA: How many girls have you ever told that to?

EUSTACE: None!

ANNETTA: I'll bet you had a lot of girls crazy for you... in your home town....

EUSTACE: Well...

ANNETTA: It's really none of my business what you did before me, is it? But I'll bet you knew a lot of girls.... (*She sits on stool.*)

EUSTACE: It was a small town. I guess you could say I knew a few pople.

ANNETTA: White girls, too?

EUSTACE: Let's get that out the way. You heard that back fence talk too. Well, 'tain't true. No white man chased me 'way from my home. I let folks think whatever they want 'cause 'tain't none of they business an' 'tain't none of mine what they thinking. I come up here after my mamma died.

ANNETTA: I didn't know.

EUSTACE: Don't go feelin' sorry for her. I was happy
when that old lady died....

ANNETTA: Happy?

EUSTACE: Hear that? I called her "old lady" ...even
though she was only fourteen years older'n me. But
damn, she looked so old. Died 'cause she was old.
Worked so hard that she just couldn't wake up when
the fire started. Time we got her out, she was... (*He
sits left of* ANNETTA.) well, she live three days with us
puttin' every kinda grease on her we could get. Butter!
Lard! Grease, you know! Fannin' her. And her sufferin'
so much. Too much! Her eyes...they was burned
open...and she just seem to keep lookin' at me. Just
lookin'. Then when all the neighbors left for the night, I
put a pillow 'cross her face...and let her go...

(ANNETTA *gasps.*)

EUSTACE: Now see, I didn't want to get on that. Had it
at the back of my mind where it belong. All I wanted
to do was tell you the truth 'bout why I come up here.
Anyway, after Mama pass, my Aunt Lizzie told me she
could use some help with the store since Uncle Anse
had passed...and I come! No! No white man chased
me 'way from my home. Now, we ain't gonna talk on
that no more. We gotta spend all our little bit of time
together being happy with each other.

(LIZZIE *crosses left exit up stairs to roof.*)

ANNETTA: Eustace...?

EUSTACE: Yeah?

ANNETTA: What you did...for your mother I mean....

EUSTACE: Yeah?

ANNETTA: It was a brave thing...a loving thing. I don't
care what anyone might say....

EUSTACE: Me neither...but thanks...

ANNETTA: Kiss me.

(ANNETTA *winces.* EUSTACE *apologizes…. He then timidly kisses her. She overwhelms him with her aggressiveness….* LIZZIE *opens door, then closes it.)*

EUSTACE: Hot damn.

ANNETTA: I knew it. I knew this would be how it felt. I just knew it.

EUSTACE: Oh, Netta, Netta.

ANNETTA: You don't think I'm being too bold, do you?

EUSTACE: No…No….

ANNETTA: And you'll always be nice to me…?

EUSTACE: I'm gonna see to it that you never have no more unhappy days. Oh, baby, I love you.

ANNETTA: Oh…me too…but we gotta be careful somebody might come up…

EUSTACE: Let'em.

ANNETTA: No. We have to be careful.

EUSTACE: Netta, don't cool me down. I'm up, I'm way up.

LIZZIE: *(She enters onto roof crosses right.)* Well you'd better get down….

EUSTACE: Damn, Aunt Lizzie. *(He stands crosses left.)*

LIZZIE: Eustace, go'n downstairs…her father's comin'.

ANNETTA: He is? *(She crosses left takes basket.)* I wonder how come my brothers…?

LIZZIE: Don't just stand there, boy. Go on downstairs.

EUSTACE: Okay! Netta when we gonna get together.

ANNETTA: Soon…I'll think of something….

LIZZIE: Yeah…if it's in the cards the game'll get played. You want to get her and yourself in trouble again.

EUSTACE: I'm goin'. 'Bye 'Netta.

ANNETTA: 'Bye.

(EUSTACE *exit hall.*)

ANNETTA: Thank you Mrs Harris.

LIZZIE: Just a minute, Miss Fast…you ain't got me fooled by a long shot…I seen you…heatin' him up… coolin' him down…. Playin' him like you the great big fisherman and he the mudskipper. If you think I can't see through you, you need dustin '. He's a big, country boy.

(EUSTACE *enters hall from roof crosses right exits* LIZZIE *apartment.*)

LIZZIE: I love him and you ain't gonna hurt him.…

ANNETTA: What makes you think I want to hurt him?

LIZZIE: He ain't all that innocent but you something new to him…. You different. He ain't used to your kind. He need his own kind.

ANNETTA: What kind am I, Mrs Harris? *(She puts basket down.)* What are we fighting for? You love him and so do I…and don't tell me I don't know anything about love because I'll be the first to admit I don't. But I know this, the first day I saw him I said to myself, "this is the one". I want him. You're talking about his kind of girls…like some of them that live on this block? Well you take a look at 'em…I'm not the prettiest by any means…but Eustace doesn't know that…and look at this. *(She shows her back.)*

LIZZIE: Oh, God, child.

ANNETTA: Which one of those girls would go through this to have him.… They just don't have it.…

LIZZIE: I know your father whipped up on you, child… but I didn't know it was anything like that. Listen, if you still bound on him after this, y'all come to my place. You can meet there as well as up here.

ANNETTA: Thank you...but no. I don't care what I have to do to have him...and if he wants me, he's going to have to risk a little too...but it's no sense getting everyone in trouble...I'll figure things out as we go along.

LIZZIE: Eustace think you a sweet young thing. Lordie! You been here before 'cause you sure act like you older'n anybody's eighteen.

(NIMROD *enters from down stage room crosses right into hall exit up steps to roof.*)

LIZZIE: He don't really know what he gettin' into do he? Poor thing.

(SOLOMON *enters from down stage room, crosses right into hall exit up steps to roof.*)

LIZZIE: Hah! I hope the day don't come too soon when these men realize how we got to work'em so they can just be somethin'.

(LIZZIE *and* ANNETTA *embrace.*)

ANNETTA: I knew you'd understand.

NIMROD: (*He enters roof.*) Where's Eustace.

(ANNETTA *shrugs her shoulders.*)

NIMROD: Papa's coming.

ANNETTA: (*She crosses left to basket.*) I know that....

NIMROD: (*He crosses down right on roof.*) How you know? He ain't cross Tenth Avenue yet....

SOLOMON: (*He enters roof crosses up right.*) I spotted him.

ANNETTA: (*To* LIZZIE) You said he was already...

LIZZIE: I knew you'd understand. 'Bye now. (*She exits roof.*)

NIMROD: What were you two gabbin' 'bout?

ANNETTA: Women's talk...! Too much for you two to even try to think about! Go on down.

(ANNETTA *gives* NIMROD *basket.*)

ANNETTA: If he asks where I am, tell him.

(ANNETTA *crosses right sits on stool.* NIMROD *and* SOLOMON *exit roof.* LIZZIE *enters down roof steps crosses right exit thru her apartment door.*)

(Out)

(Some evenings later)

(BARTON *is drying his feet after having soaked them in the beef brine. The clothesline is soaking in the tub.* FLORIE *at oval table lights match; lights lamp.* FLORIE *is knitting... after drying his feet and putting on his shoes...*BARTON *wrings out the ropes and hangs them on the wall to dry....*)

(FLORIE *crosses up right center opens apartment door, crosses left to wall cupboard opens, takes out glass.*)

BARTON: Florie, I have decided that Annetta will marry Wallace.

(FLORIE *crosses left to icebox.*)

BARTON: What do you think about that?

FLORIE: When will you tell Annetta?

BARTON: When it's time.

FLORIE: *(She crosses right to up center above table.)* And when will that be Joseph. What is the proper time to tell a young woman that her life is being arranged for her.

BARTON: It's only fit and proper that we find someone. We have daughters and have the obligation.

FLORIE: Then why aren't *we* finding a husband for Agnes? She's the eldest.

BARTON: Agnes has the head to become a person of responsibility. She could command a decent salary. She could end up as a private secretary.

FLORIE: So she won't need a husband?

BARTON: We're not discussing Agnes. We're speaking of Annetta.

FLORIE: Oh, yes. *(She crosses left to icebox.)* I forgot. Well, Joseph, *(She opens icebox, takes out pitcher, pours glass of water.)* I don't think Annetta will like the idea.

BARTON: And who is Annetta to like or dislike?

FLORIE: Joseph, this is 1927. We're in modern times. Girls don't want their husbands chosen for them. *(She crosses up center leaves pitcher glass on top icebox.)* ...not even our girls.

BARTON: That's enough woman . I won't discuss it anymore.

FLORIE: Girls want love while they're young.

BARTON: Love. What is love? Can you buy bread with it? Will it pay rent? What can it do? I'll tell you what love is. Love is two people without a thought to the future...without a look at the past. They don't care where they come from and don't give a farthing where they're going. They talk about silly things. The moon! The stars! The heavens! Bah! Saying asinine things like, "I thank God for you." Rubbish! Who is God? Who's seen him? You? *(He puts on and ties shoe.)* Then come the babies...conceived in drunkenness...and fevered passions. Unprepared for! Unthought of as a natural outcome of lunatic alli ances. Unwanted! Their futures assured beneath lampposts...either shooting craps or awaiting the next customer. *(He rolls pants leg down.)* Look out that window and hear the frantic bleatings of those with the razor scars across their cheeks. They are in, as you call it, love! *(He takes pipe and matches.)* That's young and irresponsible love!

FLORIE: I've never had love. All I ever had was you.

(BARTON lights pipe.)

BARTON: If you were dissatisfied, you should have registered your complaints. I gave as I was given.

FLORIE: I took what I got...to my shame. So I guess you have to tell me what it was all for. Every time you would put me beneath you and begin to batter me so, I would wonder why I had to hurt so much. Where was the ecstacy my girl friends told me would be there? You would loom over me with a smile on your lips, and then come into me, filling me with yourself. I would wonder "why isn't the man kissing me?" You see I was young enough to think that trivial things like kissing and loving went hand in hand....

BARTON: You have waited until now to take leave of your senses. *(He puts pipe down.)* We were united together because your parents sensibly decided what was best for you... *(He takes glasses off, puts in case, puts case in vest pocket.)* because they knew that you, like most girls, didn't know...and they knew that I had brains. Ambition! Ideas!

FLORIE: Ah, yes. Ideas. The children would rebuild our glorious past. The children were going to be the new beginning of Africa. I believed in you. I felt like a saint carrying the new nation within me. How fortunate I was to have been chosen. It was only after the children started coming one after another...like steps, Joseph... that I realized they were quite ordinary children. And when the last three passed on, I knew it for sure. They died like quite ordinary children...no different from other children right here on 63rd street. Quite ordinary children and I was a stupid...less than ordinary woman. So you tell me…Joseph. Tell me what it was all for.

(BARTON *stands crosses left into apartment hall to coatrack.*)

FLORIE: If you can't, then I'll just have to believe that I bore those two girls to be bartered away. The one for her brains…

(BARTON *puts on jacket and hat.*)

FLORIE: …and the money you think she can bring you…and the other to be a prisoner in a bed with a man you designate as substitute because before God, whom you fear despite…

(BARTON *crosses right to apartment door.*)

FLORIE: …what you say, you can't be in that bed yourself.

(BARTON *turns faces* FLORIE. LIZZIE *crosses into hall.*)

BARTON: How dare you…

(AGNES *and* ANNETTA *enter from up stage room crosses down thru arch.*)

BARTON: Get back inside!

(AGNES *and* ANNETTA *cross to up stage room doorway, stand.*)

BARTON: How dare you! How dare you befoul my home with your vile mouth. You disgrace me. You disgrace your family…you disgrace your people. (*He crosses to* FLORIE *raising hand to strike her.*) You disgrace all that is decent.

FLORIE: Go ahead. Why don't you strike me? After all these years it would be a relief.

BARTON: (*Bellowing*) Annetta! Annetta! (*He crosses down center.*) Annetta! Come out here.

ANNETTA: Mama?

(ANNETTA *crosses down left center.* FLORIE *crosses left leans on icebox.*)

BARTON: I have decided you will marry Mr Wallace. I want no discussion...no back sass. Now, go!

ANNETTA: I won't! I'll kill myself before I do!

(AGNES *exits up stage room.*)

BARTON: You'll have ample opportunity to demonstrate the strength of your threat. Go to your room.

ANNETTA: No!

FLORIE: Go, Annetta. Go, damn it, go!

(ANNETTA *goes to her room.*)

BARTON: I'll be returning late.

(LIZZIE *crosses right stand beside chair, looks out window.* BARTON *crosses up right center exits apartment, crosses exits down steps.* LIZZIE *sits in chair.*)

BARTON: You need not wait.

(FLORIE *puts pitcher in icebox, takes glass, crosses up center to sink, places glass in sink, crosses right to sewing basket, places basket on trunk, takes shirt out—examines it, puts shirt in basket crosses up right center opens apartment door.*)

LIZZIE: Hi, Florie:

FLORIE: Oh, Lizzie. I didn't even see you there....

LIZZIE: I'm easy to miss when you got so much on your mind....

FLORIE: You heard?

LIZZIE: Hard not to.

(LIZZIE *stands takes chair, crosses left, places chair right of door opening.* FLORIE *sits in chair.* LIZZIE *crosses right into apartment, returns with another chair places right center [spike marks].*)

FLORIE: You remember when you were eighteen?

LIZZIE: Well now...it ain't been that long.

FLORIE: Remember the feeling in your blood...?

LIZZIE: Blood don't change, honey. It's still there. Lord God! I had just seen Anse for the first. That big, shiny, black nigger come walkin' up the road on a hot day... with his shirt sleeves rolled up...that can do it for me, you know. Love to see me a black man with his shirt sleeves rolled up and, Lord, don't let the shirt be white...wooeee! Anyway he comes up the road... just stridin'...ain't lookin' left...ain't lookin' right. Just knowin' every eye was on him. Well, Florie, I fell. I really fell. It was so hot...I was so hot.... The sight of him and them shirt sleeves set my blood to boilin' and my little pupee to twitchin'...I just fell right out...right out in front of him....

FLORIE: You ain't mean it.

(FLORIE *and* LIZZIE *laugh.*)

LIZZIE: For true, girl. For true. He pick me up and took me down to the creek and threw some water in my face. When I open my eyes and saw him leanin' over me...I give him some right there on the bank. Didn't particularly give a good goddamn who saw me, and left town with him that day.

FLORIE: You must have really been happy....

LIZZIE: Happy? Happy's too simple a word. You know, before be passed.... Life wasn't all roses. Can't be when a man look like him and there's other gals sniffin . He could make me downright miserable when he wanted to but, shit, I'd go through it all again. Ain't had no other. Ain't want no other. Ain't need no other...and ain't no other 'round to make me forget him. Aw, Florie, you had the feelin'....

FLORIE: Once…back home. There was a young black god. I wanted to… It's spilled milk. My parents decided Joseph was for my own good. Oh well, he's probably still there. He had not the slightest bit of ambition. Anyway…Annetta's my concern now.

LIZZIE: I know what run through her head when she see Eustace.

FLORIE: I do too…and I wish it was running through her head…but it's in her body…in her blood. If she was using her head she'd be able to see the rocks in the road…and if I were using mine, I'd tell her.

LIZZIE: I seen 'em together and them rocks don't mean shit. Florie, they both strainin' and chompin' to get over them rocks so they can get at each other.

FLORIE: So?

LIZZIE: So…let 'em go, if you got the grit…throw 'em together….

FLORIE: Things could get out of hand.

LIZZIE: They in hand now, I suppose? How many times you done lay awake wishin' you had that young West Indian boy back home layin' next to you? How many times you had to put his face on top your man's face so you could pretend you was enjoyin' it? I know it's risky…but hell…that's life in a nutshell…risks….

FLORIE: Where would they go? Your house?

LIZZIE: No! She told me she'd never use me that way.

FLORIE: She told you…?

LIZZIE: Girl, we done talked. Let 'em go to the roof. That's where they been goin'.

FLORIE: What?

LIZZIE: Little stolen time to be with each other for a while…not enough time to do doodledeesquat. Lemme go get him and send him on up.

(FLORIE *stands crosses up stage left to roof steps.*)

FLORIE: (*After some deliberation. She crosses to up stage of left chair.*) All right…I'm doing the right thing, aren't I? She wants the delirium. All right…

(LIZZIE *stands crosses into her apartment with her chair. Crosses left to* FLORIE)

FLORIE: …let her have it before the dullness sets in. I am doing the right thing, aren't I?

LIZZIE: Unless you got somethin' else up your sleeve. Aw, Florie. Go talk to her and tell her…and who knows…maybe we can bury all this silly ass West Indian-nigger shit where it belongs…

(FLORIE *crosses left into her apartment.* LIZZIE *closes her apartment, exits down steps to street.*)

FLORIE: (*She crosses left to up stage arch.*) Annetta! Come here…I want to talk to you.

(AGNES *and* ANNETTA *enter from up stage room.*)

ANNETTA: Yes, ma'am.

FLORIE: Just Annetta, Agnes.

(AGNES *crosses up stage stands in doorway up stage room. They close the bedroom door. She goes to the door of the male bed room.*)

FLORIE: Either of you two have to go to the toilet?

NIMROD: Not me!

SOLOMON: No!

FLORIE: Good…stay in your room…I'll be busy out here… (*She closes that door.*) Annetta, wipe your eyes and sit here.

(FLORIE *and* ANNETTA *crosses right below table.* ANNETTA *sits stage right table chair.*)

FLORIE: Crying is for girls and you have to grow up now. *(She crosses right below oval table.)* You are to go up to the roof.

ANNETTA: The roof?

FLORIE: Don't interrupt. Someone will be coming up to meet you...

ANNETTA: Eustace?

FLORIE: It may be wrong what I'm doing. I pray to God. It's not. But I'm not going to let you end up like me... without ever having one crazy dream come true. So you go up there...go and meet your boy.

ANNETTA: He's a man, Mama.

FLORIE: Not yet, baby. *(She crosses left to* ANNETTA.*)* You're not a woman either but you go up to the roof and don't come down until you are. Now go and don't worry about things here... Go! ...Go! ...Go before I start to think....

(ANNETTA *kisses* FLORIE, *stands, crosses up right center to door exits up stairs to roof.* FLORIE *sinks to her knees. She looks out window,* AGNES *crosses into room stands up stage arch.*)

FLORIE: They always told me you guided our every move good and bad...I hope it's true...and I hope you know what you're doing....

(AGNES *has been listening and comes over to* FLORIE.*)*

AGNES: I hope the both of you know what you're doing.... *(She crosses down right center to* FLORIE.*)*

FLORIE: You're a very sensible girl, Agnes. I hope for your sake you don't stay that way I'd like to think that when a piece of life offers itself to you...you not only taste it...but eat it down until you pass it out the next day. *(She blows out hurricane lamp. She crosses into archway.)*

(Out)

(Much later that evening, BARTON enters the dark apartment from street, crosses up left center to stove takes box of matches crosses up right, places cane on chair. Crosses down right center to oval table, trips on brine.)

BARTON: ARTCH!

(NIMROD and SOLOMON enter down stage room crosses into kitchen.)

NIMROD: Papa, that you?

BARTON: Who else lives here? Why was not this brine put away?

(NIMROD and SOLOMON cross right to brine; lift, crosses with brine, places up center to right of sink. NIMROD puts cover on brine.)

NIMROD: We didn't know it was still out.

SOLOMON: We went to bed early.

NIMROD: You told us to, Papa…

(NIMROD crosses right picks towel off floor crosses up center places on top of brine. BARTON lights lamp.)

NIMROD: …so we could get up early for the parade in the morning.

(NIMROD and SOLOMON cross left to arch.)

BARTON: Aha! Well, come here…both of you.

(SOLOMON cross down table to left of table.)

NIMROD: Hunh? I mean…yes, sir?

BARTON: Sit! …Sit…sit…sit. On second thought, Solomon you go into my chest and bring me my brandy. Nimrod, fetch three glasses. No need to look at each other so balefully. You did nothing wrong.

Do you so fear your father, that when he makes the slightest request of you, you tremble?

NIMROD: It's just that it's so late, Papa.

BARTON: Do as I say, both of you.

(SOLOMON *cross left exits down stage room* NIMROD *crosses up left center to cupboard takes out three shot glasses.* BARTON *crosses up left center to stove places matches on stove shelf.* SOLOMON *enters from down stage room with decanter of brandy.* BARTON *takes brandy, gives* SOLOMON *his hat.* SOLOMON *crosses left puts hat on coat rack.*)

BARTON: Now, sit!

(BARTON *crosses up center table.* NIMROD *crosses sits stage left table chair.* SOLOMON *crosses right sits stage right table chair.*)

BARTON: I am going to pour each of you a little of this and will toast your very good health...tonight I have concluded a piece of business that will not only help us as a family...but as a nation of people.

NIMROD: What was that?

BARTON: It is two years now since Garvey was in carcerated, correct? Yet every Sunday...rain or shine...I make you put on your helmets and march with me throughout the neighborhood. You hate to put on those helmets and carry the placards and march with me and the others. Is this not so?

SOLOMON: We don't hate...

BARTON: Nonsense! I've repeatedly asked you not to lie to me. Why do you hate to march with...

NIMROD: It's not that we hate the marching...but people laugh at us....

BARTON: And who are these people who laugh at us?

NIMROD: All our friends we go to school with. They're always calling us stuck-up, crazy monkey-chasers, tinheads…and other things.

BARTON: Your friends, you say, call you these names?

NIMROD: Yes.

SOLOMON: Papa…don't you hear 'em when we're marching.

BARTON: No, son. I don 't hear them. I never hear them because there are stronger voices that shout in my ears. If you would only listen most carefully, you would hear them as they drown out those pitiful bleats from your "friends"…as you call them. Garvey screams in my ears. Africa roars… *(He crosses right to oval table with lamp.)* bellows, "bring my people home!" You think I always had contempt for the Americans? No, Not true. Marcus and I came here with our hearts open to receive and to give. Where was there a bigger concentration of black people who needed enlightenment and inspiration to go back to the land robbed from us? *(He places lamp on table.)* …Where was there a greater gathering of rhythm to underscore the cadence of our marching feet as we took back what was ours before they took us? We thought it was here… and for a while it seemed true. We have only a handful to march tomorrow…but you should have seen us then. Hundreds swelled to thousands. People had never seen such black numbers. Indeed it came as a surprise to many of our own people that we numbered so many. Is it any wonder that our power awed and put fear into those who watched in silence? It wasn't to be long before they were setting the traps. It was to be even shorter until they sprung them. Devious and dedicated forces went to work against us…paving their way and corrupting from within. Lies were told…and lies were believed. Marcus was toppled by a power far

greater...far greener...far whiter...far blacker than any
there could be in those heavens above...and before our
ship of hope could sail...it sank into chasms far deeper
than the deepest abyss. A few of us tried a resurrection
but to no avail...the harpoons had been driven in
securely and did their work. We ran into walls of
black indifference and contented ignorance. We are
trapped in this land with a people...who were almost
ours. People, who when the water got hot...preferred
to leap from the kettle. That's why I cannot relax...
nor can I allow you to relax. You must, at all times,
hold yourselves to not be treated as these people have
allowed themselves to be. The power of your brain will
mark you apart. The power of your brain will get you
home to Africa...and there you will be masters. Your
sisters will be queens and fortify the land. And should
a man from another race come into your kingdom
and dare to cross your sisters...or cross you...or cross
your threshold without your consent... *(He crosses up
right center to door.)* ...you will beat him down and take
what is left of his carcass and nail it to your door as
a warning to all who would dare try this again... *(He
crosses to up center of table.)* Remember having a black
skin is not a curse. Being in this country with a black
skin is a curse. You are different... *(He crosses left to
right to oval table.)* ...and when people laugh at you
for being so...your affirmations shouted at the tops of
your lungs to the tops of the world shall drown them...
are you listening?

SOLOMON: Yes...yes, sir.

(NIMROD has drifted off to sleep...)

BARTON: *(He crosses left to up left table, slaps NIMROD.)*
Fool! I will not let you slip back...will go back to Africa
if I have to walk across your back to get there.... Go to
the room...both of you...

(NIMROD *and* SOLOMON *cross left, exit to down stage room.* BARTON *crosses right to oval table, takes lamp, crosses left to up stage arch.*)

BARTON: No, Mr Eustace Baylor…your people have destroyed one dream…you shan't wake me from another. *(He exits down stage room with lamp.)*

(FLORIE *comes out and seats herself in the now darkened apartment.*)

(Out)

(EUSTACE *and* ANNETTA *embrace.* EUSTACE *crosses down center, sits.*)

EUSTACE: I'm thinkin' shouldn't hold you to me no more. Maybe you should do like your pa want and only see that West Indian nigger. Least he could show you some places. Goddamn, 'Netta…I can't even show you off . Don't nobody know I belong to you.

ANNETTA: Eustace, *(She crosses to right of* EUSTACE.*)* this roof is all the world I need. You 're here. I don't have to tell anybody or show anybody that I belong to you. I just do. That's all. I know it. You know it. And when I walk down the street and people see my face…they know it. *(She sits.)* You don't have to be with me to be with me. You're like God…just everywhere I go. And the look in my eyes shows you off.

(EUSTACE *and* ANNETTA *embrace.*)

EUSTACE: Every time we manage to get together, you work me up. Then you cool me down. Up! Down! Up and down! You playin' me again. 'Netta.

ANNETTA: No. I'm never going to play again.

EUSTACE: You sure? You ain't just funnin' me?

ANNETTA: I love you, Eustace. I'm going to give all my love to you. I want you to give all your love to me. I never want you to love anyone else but me. I don't want children because I don't ever want to share you. And I'll never let you die because I won't even share you with God.

EUSTACE: Oh, 'Netta...

ANNETTA: Ssssh, baby. It's time. *(She unbuttons blouse.)*

(Out)

END OF ACT TWO

ACT THREE

(It's December. There's a wreath on LIZZIE'S *door.)*

*(*AGNES *sits stage right in* FLORIE'S *chair correcting papers.*
NIMROD *sits ottoman reading homebound book.* ANNETTA
at stove stirring soup.)

*(*ANNETTA *crosses left exit to toilet, down stage of down
stage room.)*

NIMROD: You going to the toilet again? *(He stands
crosses left to arch.)* Doggone, girl, you spend more time
in there lately than the law allows...

AGNES: *(She stands crosses left to stove, covers soup.)* Why
don't you keep quiet?

NIMROD: What'd I say...? Doggone...hey...wash
your hands...before you come out...I don't want you
serving my food with...

AGNES: You're far from funny...

*(*ANNETTA *goes into the toilet.)*

NIMROD: Why don't you dry up? That's right you can't
dry up no more than you are.

*(*SOLOMON *enters hall, up steps, crosses left enter
apartment. Closes door throws books on floor)*

NIMROD: Great valentino! What war you been in.

*(*SOLOMON *crosses left to arch.* NIMROD *stops him.)*

SOLOMON: Listen. Don't start no shit...and there won't be none.

NIMROD: Who the fuck you talkin' to, nigger?

(SOLOMON *crosses right, crosses down table, crosses left.*)

NIMROD: What in the fuck is wrong with you lately.

(SOLOMON *crosses right sits* FLORIE's *chair.*)

NIMROD: Can't nobody say shit to you without you nastyin' off. Whoever kicked your ass probably had damn good reason.

SOLOMON: Ain' nobody kicked my ass....

NIMROD: Yeah, I know. (*He crosses right to up left of oval table.*) "You shoulda seen the other guy." Well, you better watch it. You gonna go off on the wrong person and I'm gonna haf ta kick your ass....

SOLOMON: You and what army?

AGNES: (*She crosses to cabinet. Takes face cloth from drawer.*) If the two of you don't stop it, I'm gonna hafta kick both your asses. You sound just like street niggers. (*She crosses up center to sink wets facecloth.*)

SOLOMON: You mean Americans? (*He crosses left to* AGNES.) Why don't you say what you mean?

AGNES: (*She crosses down to roof of table.*) What is wrong with you Solomon?

SOLOMON: Just sick and tired of it. Sick and tired of havin' to fight all the time just to prove that I'm just as good as anybody else....

NIMROD: (*He crosses left to right of* SOLOMON.) Why you keep lettin' that old shit upset you?

SOLOMON: I beat up Willie Clay today! My best friend!

NIMROD: For what, man?

SOLOMON: He called me a "West Indian fuck." I beat him up....

(AGNES *sits.* SOLOMON, *stage right table chair, cleans blood from his face.*)

SOLOMON: We went down by the pier...we went there right after school.

(NIMROD *crosses right sits* FLORIE *chair.*)

SOLOMON: We were just sitting there. We got around to talkin' 'bout Christmas comin' and I started sayin' how I wish we could keep Christmas but Papa don't believe in it. It being a white man's holiday and all... and he said "aw shit...if that's all that's botherin' you, I already got you a Christmas present...you West Indian fuck." I hit him. I jumped all over him, he hardly had a chance to hit back. I just beat him up. My best friend. When are we going back to Africa? I want to go now! Right now! I hate 63rd Street! I hate it!

(ANNETTA *cornes out of the toilet.*)

AGNES: 63rd Street isn't the whole world .

SOLOMON: It is! It's the whole, entire world. 'Till we get to Africa like Papa says.

NIMROD: Africa? Shit! Use your head for something else 'sides a hatrack (*He stands crosses left to right of* SOLOMON.) Garvey's ass in jail and Papa ain't goin' nowhere 'cept marching with a handful of West Indians up and down 63rd to 64th Street. We don't even cross 10th Avenue to the Irish and Italian sections. Ain't none of us ever gonna reach no Africa. You and me gotta do our damnedest to be Americans because Papa and Mama gonna die here. Annetta will marry Mr Wallace after she graduates next month. Agnes gonna make out 'cause she got brains and gonna be a secretary. What do you and I do? We born here, damn it...and have to prove that we're as good as they are.

(SOLOMON *stands crosses left below table, exit down stage roorn.*)

AGNES: No! You're better.

NIMROD: That's Papa talking. We're as good. We're as bad. Can't nobody understand we just wanna be the same? (*He crosses left, above table, exit down stage roorn.*) The same God damn it! (*He goes into the toilet.*)

(ANNETTA *enters frorn toilet.* AGNES *crosses up center puts cloth in sink.*)

FLORIE: (*From within*) What's going on out there?

(AGNES *crosses left to up stage arch.*)

AGNES: Nothing Mama, try and go back to sleep.

FLORIE: (*From within*) I'll be out shortly.

ANNETTA: (*She crosses up left center to stove, stirs soup.*) What was that all about?

AGNES: (*She takes up stage chair, crosses right, places down right table.*) Couldn't you guess?

ANNETTA: No and I couldn 't care less…

AGNES: I guess you do have other things on your mind.

ANNETTA: Meaning?

AGNES: (*She crosses up right center to* BARTON *chair, crosses up center table places* BARTON *chair.*) I guess I wouldn't notice my brothers face was bloody either if I had your problem. You could at least pretend you're having your period. Does Mama know, you think?

ANNETTA: I wouldn't doubt it. Mama's not dumb.

AGNES: (*She crosses up right center to ottoman, crosses down right places ottoman on spike mark to right of oval table.*) Are you going to marry him?

ANNETTA: I suppose I'll have to.

AGNES: What do you mean…you suppose.

ANNETTA: I meant to say, "yes".

AGNES: *(She crosses up right to* FLORIE's *chair, crosses left places chair down center table.)* Papa will kill you...

ANNETTA: Papa better not ever put his bands on me again. I mean it.

AGNES: You're thinking Eustace will stop him? Hah! *(She crosses up right to trunk.)* Well you wanted him.

ANNETTA: And I got him too, didn't I?

AGNES: *(She takes folder and typing papers, sits.)* You don't sound too thrilled.

ANNETTA: *(She crosses right to trunk.)* I just didn't think it was going to go this far. I hadn't really thought I'd get to marriage so soon.

AGNES: *(She puts paper in folder.)* What had you planned to do about Mr Wallace next month ?

ANNETTA: I would have thought of something. *(She sits on trunk.)* I guess something would have come up.

AGNES: Something did come up and it appears to be you. When do you plan to break the news to...

ANNETTA: I plan to tell Mama first. Then I'll tell Papa when we're eating. I have it all planned. Don't worry.

AGNES: Good. However, I was referring to your fiance...Mr Wallace.

ANNETTA: Papa can tell him. He's more his fiance than mine.

AGNES: None of this is his fault, you know. He worships Papa so. That's the only reason be consented to Papa's arrangement...but maybe it's best I tell him... maybe he won't take it so hard....

ANNETTA: Agnes! Well I'll be damned. Why didn't you say something?

AGNES: If I ever marry, it won't just be for love. Love get your ass in all sorts of trouble.

(FLORIE *enters from up stage room, yawning, crossing down stands up stage arch.*)

FLORIE: What are you ladies chattering about? The food smells good, Annetta. (*She crosses up left center to stove.*)

(BARTON *enters up steps with package in hand, crosses left to door.*)

ANNETTA: Mama… (*She stands crosses left to* FLORIE.) I have to talk to you…

FLORIE: What about?

(BARTON *opens apartment door, enters.*)

ANNETTA: Oh, nothing. It can wait until later.

BARTON: Good evening.

FLORIE, ANNETTA & AGNES: Good evening.

(ANNETTA *crosses left to above oval table,* FLORIE *crosses to* BARTON. *Takes hat crosses left places on coat rack.*)

(NIMROD *and* SOLOMON *enter from down stage room, cross right to table,* NIMROD *up stage chair,* SOLOMON *down stage chair.*)

NIMROD & SOLOMON: Good evening Papa.

BARTON: Yes.

NIMROD: We were washing up for dinner.

BARTON: The package is for Annetta .

(ANNETTA *crosses up to* BARTON *takes package.*)

BARTON: You may open it. It's your wedding dress.

(AGNES *crosses left to* BARTON *takes coat crosses left hangs coat on coat rack.* FLORIE *crosses right to right of oval table.*)

ANNETTA: I'll open it later. (*She crosses right places package on oval table.*) Dinner's ready.

BARTON: I want you to open it now. Is it everyday
you get a wedding dress? It was of some expense, you
know. *(He places cane up center chair at table crosses up
center to sink washes hands.)* I had thought both of you
ladies would be married in the same dress as your
mother, but I couldn't find it in the trunk where it used
to be....

FLORIE: If you had asked, I would have told you. I
made up a package and sent it home years ago.

BARTON: *(He crosses down stage to up of table drying
hands.)* Why would you send your wedding dress back
home?

FLORIE: I want my daughters to find their own
happiness...and not duplicate mine.

BARTON: *(He tosses cloth into sink, crosses to iip center
table chair, sits.)* Annetta, what about the soup?

ANNETTA: *(She crosses up left center to stove, ladles soup
into bowls.)* Coming just now.

BARTON: Be quick about it. Agnes, what about today?

AGNES: *(She crosses to left of BARTON.)* I stayed home
today Papa...I wasn't at all well. I had...

BARTON: I did not ask you the nature of your
complaint.

FLORIE: *(She crosses left sits down center chair at table.)*
Don't forget to take some senna tea before you go to
bed.

BARTON: Nimrod, what about today?

NIMROD: Okay!

BARTON: Okay! What is okay!

NIMROD: Everything went well. Nothing extraordi-
nary.

SOLOMON: It's the same with me.

BARTON: Had I asked you ?

(ANNETTA *takes bowl of soup crosses down to left of*
BARTON, *places soup on table in front of* BARTON, *crosses
to stove.* AGNES *takes two bowls soup, crosses down places
in front of* NIMROD *then* SOLOMON; *crosses to stove.*
ANNETTA *takes two bowls soup, crosses down left of table,
places one front of* FLORIE, *places one down right table sits
down right table.* AGNES *takes bowl crosses right sits up
right table.)*

ANNETTA: The soup is ready.

BARTON: We will continue this after supper.

(The family begins to eat. LIZZIE *enters from her apartment
crosses left to* BARTON *apartment door. Turns crosses
right as* EUSTACE *enters from her apartment crosses left to*
LIZZIE.)

LIZZIE: I shoulda had another swig of courage before
we go in there....

EUSTACE: You don't need it. *(He crosses left to* BARTON
apartment door.) C'mon and let's get it over with...if
you don't want to, I can handle it.

LIZZIE: No...I feel partly to blame. Ain't nobody to
blame but me.

(LIZZIE *crosses to right of* EUSTACE. *He knocks on the door.)*

SOLOMON: I'll bet that's Mr Wallace.

BARTON: Nonse! Wallace knows what time we're at
table. He wouldn't visit during this hour. Whoever
else it might be can wait out there or return later. Now,
silence!

(ANNETTA *stands, pushes chair under table.* EUSTACE
knocks again.)

BARTON: Return to your seat, young woman.

(ANNETTA *crosses up right center to apartment door.*
Ignoring him ANNETTA *opens door.* LIZZIE *and* EUSTACE
enter. LIZZIE *crosses left center to left of table* EUSTACE
crosses up center above BARTON.)

FLORIE: Dear God.

(BARTON *ignores the visitors.*)

LIZZIE: 'Evenin' Florie. Y'all 'scuse us for bustin' in on
y'alls dinner but...

BARTON: Solomon, stop staring. Close your mouth and
pay attention to your soup.

LIZZIE: Like I said...we didn't mean to interrupt your
dinner.

EUSTACE: Hold on, Aunt Lizzie. Let me...

ANNETTA: *(Cautioning.)* Eustace... *(She crosses right
to left of* BARTON.) Papa, I'm not...I can't marry Mr
Wallace. Eustace and I are having a baby.

(EUSTACE *crosses to left of* ANNETTA.)

ANNETTA: I'm pregnant!

EUSTACE: I want us to get married Sunday next at Saint
Cyprian's.

(FLORIE *stands sends* NIMROD *and* SOLOMON *to room;
crosses right to left of oval table. Boys stand cross left to
arch.*)

FLORIE: ...My poor baby. What have I done.

ANNETTA: *(She crosses right to* FLORIE.) I didn't want it
to come out like that...so cold. I wanted to say it in a
nice way. What I mean is I did want to say it like that
but I'm sorry I did...I don't know what...

EUSTACE: You don't have to 'pologize.

ANNETTA: Eustace...please...

(Silence)

LIZZIE: We can have the weddin' celebration at my house right after . *(To* BARTON*)* I know it ain't likely but you welcome to come...if you wanna. *(She crosses up right center to apartment door.)*

ANNETTA: Papa, say something...please.

*(*BARTON *stands crosses left center to rope, hanging left of cupboard.)*

FLORIE: No!

*(*FLORIE *crosses to left of* ANNETTA*.* AGNES *stands crosses to right of* ANNETTA*.* NIMROD *and* SOLOMON *step into kitchen.)*

FLORIE: ...Blame me...I told her to do it...blame me but you shan't touch her.

EUSTACE: *(He crosses to* FLORIE*.)* He ain't touchin' nobody. 'Specially 'Netta. 'Netta you get whatever you takin' 'cause you ain't stayin' here this night.... *(He crosses to up center of table.)* Listen, old man, I ain't come here to pack no trouble with you. 'Netta said she just didn't want you to...just find out....

*(*BARTON *crosses down right table rope in hand.)*

EUSTACE: Lord knows why she wanna be sparin' you after all you done to her. But that's okay 'cause I'm gonna take her 'way where I can love her away from this place away from you and your meanness. I love her. She and me is havin' this baby and ain't nothin' you can do 'bout it....

BARTON: You listen to me, abomination...

*(*LIZZIE *crosses to up left table.)*

LIZZIE: What?

BARTON: For the second time you show how unworthy you are. You people drift through life...infiltrating good people with your filthy ways...

LIZZIE: Filthy ways? Eustace don't let him talk to you that way...

BARTON: Lying! Cheating! Sneaking! Lazy! Drifting through life without cause! Going where you're not wanted! I hate you....

(BARTON crosses right to ANNETTA. FLORIE, ANNETTA, AGNES cross left to above table.)

EUSTACE: Hate me? *(He crosses right to BARTON, stage left of table.)* Is that all? I expected more than that from you...

BARTON: Maybe you understand this better...

(BARTON whips EUSTACE with rope.)

LIZZIE: *(She crosses right taking razor from pocket, crosses to right of EUSTACE.)* I'm a cut your ass, you...

(NIMROD and SOLOMON disarm LIZZIE. General chaos as BARTON continues to flail the caught-off-guard EUSTACE... who tries to protect himself.)

BARTON: Ineffectual bastard! Ineffectual bastard. Trying to destroy me...

(NIMROD and SOLOMON cross right to LIZZIE pulls her up stage takes razor from her.)

LIZZIE: Let me go, dammit! Let go me! What's wrong with you, Eustace? ...Kill him!

(EUSTACE grabs BARTON shakes him. BARTON drops rope.)

ANNETTA: Stop...Eustace...stop?

FLORIE: Oh, God. Leave off him! Leave off him.

EUSTACE: Gimp-leg motherfucker...you got no right...

(BARTON has stroke, EUSTACE lowers BARTON to floor.)

FLORIE: Oh, God...

(FLORIE crosses right below table to BARTON. At BARTON's head. NIMROD and SOLOMON cross down to EUSTACE,

pulls him off BARTON. ANNETTA *cross right below table to*
BARTON *[at* BARTON'*s feet]* . EUSTACE *grabs* ANNETTA.
NIMROD *and* SOLOMON *cross to* BARTON *side.* AGNES
cross right [above table] to BARTON *side.* LIZZIE *crosses to*
up left corner of table.)

FLORIE: …my God…Joseph…Joseph…

LIZZIE: God got him. He don't like ugly and care very
little for pretty…

AGNES: Shut up. Shut up and get out.

ANNETTA: Eustace…go!

EUSTACE: Not without you .

ANNETTA: How can I go after what you've done.

EUSTACE: After what I done…?

FLORIE: Nimmie, go for the doctor.

*(*NIMROD *crosses left, exit thru arch to down stage room.)*

FLORIE: Joseph…Joseph…don't look at me so. Close
your eyes. Die if you have to but don't look at me…so.
Annetta do something…somebody…help me.

EUSTACE: 'Netta…ain't you understand…you can't stay
here no more…

ANNETTA: Stop pulling at me…

AGNES: Didn't anyone see through to this? …Didn't
any think that something could happen?

LIZZIE: Eustace, back off. Don't you be the one to force
her…else she blame you if he dies.

*(*EUSTACE *lets* ANNETTA *go.* ANNETTA *kneels at* BARTON
feet.)

LIZZIE: Young miss, you gotta do some thinking now.
It's your man or your daddy. Florie, I'm truly sorry all
this happen. We shoulda thought this through. I'm just
sorry.

(NIMROD *enters from down stage room with coat, hat and scarf, crosses right to apartment door.*)

LIZZIE: You stay here, boy. This woman need all her family with her now. Eustace…you go get Doctor Taylor.

EUSTACE: 'Netta?

(EUSTACE *crosses to apartment exit to hall, cross right to* LIZZIE *enter her apartment. She doesn't respond.*)

LIZZIE: Go on, Eustace.

(EUSTACE *goes.* LIZZIE *goes.*)

NIMROD: *(He crosses to up right corner of table.)* Maybe we can all lift him and take him to bed….

FLORIE: No! We don't move him. Get a pillow for his head…and a blanket…

(AGNES *and* SOLOMON *cross left exit up stage room. Return:* AGNES *has pillow,* SOLOMON *has blanket.* AGNES *cross right above table to* BARTON *side.* SOLOMON *cross right below table to* BARTON *feet, up stage of* ANNETTA. FLORIE *lifts* BARTON *head.* AGNES *puts pillow under.* SOLOMON *and* AGNES *cover* BARTON *with blanket.*)

FLORIE: Gentle…

(EUSTACE *enter hall with coat and hat, exit down step to street.*)

FLORIE: …gently…gently.

(LIZZIE *closes* BARTON *door crosses right exit into her apartment.*)

(Out)

(Next Sunday, BARTON *in wheelchair pushed on stage from up right bedroom hall.* SOLOMON *has homebound book.* BARTON *has afghan over legs. Crossing stage right above table to spike marks up stage center rug.* BARTON *sits*

throughout scene staring. SOLOMON *moves table up stage of hassock. There's a peal of laughter from* LIZZIE's *apartment.)*

SOLOMON: Listen to 'em. Laughing and carrying on as if the world was still the same...can I get you anything? How about a smoke? You want yom·pipe? I'll light it for you. *(He crosses to pipe stand, takes pipe, matches, crosses right of* BARTON, *lights pipe, puffs.)* You know...it's not too bad. Still smells though. *(Places pipe in* BARTON's *mouth. More laughter)* Can you hear 'em? *(Take pipe, crosses to stand. Crosses left of* BARTON. *Places left hand in lap, crosses right to ottoman, takes book.)* They're all over there and havin' a good time. Well, I'm still here and I'm going to always be here. *(He stands crosses to left of* BARTON, *kneels.)* Look, see what I'm reading? I'm deep into the histories now...just like you always wanted. I see it all now like you said. And I got my future and the future of the people upper most in my mind. Earthly pleasures only last a minute or so. Ain't that what you mean? Well, don't you worry. I'll get us back to Africa...I don't know how but I'll do it...I'll build the nation for you. I'll do it.

*(*NIMROD *enters hall from* LIZZIE *crosses left to* BARTON *door.* SOLOMON *stands, crosses, sits on ottoman.* NIMROD *enters, crosses down steps.)*

SOLOMON: Look who's here. Tired of laughin' and havin' fun?

NIMROD: Wasn't us. There's other folks there. How's Papa? *(He crosses down right of table.)* He need anything?

SOLOMON: Ask him. Don't talk...

*(*AGNES *and* FLORIE *enter hall from* LIZZIE *crosses left to* BARTON *door.)*

SOLOMON: ...'bout him like he ain't here...)

NIMROD: Well... *(He sits right table chair.)* he can't answer nobody....

SOLOMON: It don't mean he can't hear you. And if he needs something...

(AGNES *enter* BARTON, *crosses down steps crosses right to* BARTON *kiss cheek, crosses left exit* FLORIE *room.*)

SOLOMON: ...you 'll know it. He's your·father.

(FLORIE *enters* BARTON, *close door stand landing.* SOLOMON *crosses up left to cabinet.*)

SOLOMON: Hello Mama.

FLORIE: You should have come over and at least had a piece of cake or something.

SOLOMON: I wasn't hungry...and I had a lot of studying to do... (*He opens cabinet takes cup crosses to stove pour cocoa.*)

FLORIE: You are not fooling anyone, Solomon. How ever, no matter what happens she will always be your sister. Joseph...you all right? (*She pats his hand.... She cross down steps to right to* BARTON, *adjusts blanket, crosses up left, exits room.*)

(SOLOMON *cross down right with cup, sits on ottoman.*)

NIMROD: It just don't seem right...us being over there...I should lay down...I had a drink of that stuff she makes over there...I don't like it...

(ANNETTA *enters hall from* LIZZIE *cross left to* BARTON *apartment.*)

NIMROD: ...but I guess it was only polite...my head sure feels kinda funny though. I gotta lay down.

(NIMROD *stands cross down table, cross up left exit* BARTON *room.* ANNETTA *enters* BARTON *apartment closes door.*)

(ANNETTA *cross down steps.*)

SOLOMON: Well, you all American now...?

ANNETTA: Hello Solomon. Where's Mama.

(AGNES *enters kitchen with coat and scarf from* FLORIE's *room. Crosses down left center)*

ANNETTA: How come everybody's left? Where're you going?

AGNES: Just for a walk...

FLORIE: *(To* AGNES*)* You have your scarf. It's cold out there...

AGNES: Yes...I won't be gone long.

ANNETTA: *(She crosses to* AGNES.*)* Are you coming back over?

AGNES: Maybe...Annetta, I'm sorry but I'm just not used to hanging out with that pool room crowd...

ANNETTA: I know, I'm not comfortable with them either...but they'll be going soon. You can't all just leave me over there by myself...

AGNES: Now...you think about that. I'll be back in a little while.

(AGNES *crosses right, exits door exit down hall steps.* ANNETTA *cross down left table.)*

FLORIE: *(She enters kitchen from her room cross to cabinet, takes spoon napkin from drawer, cup from cupboard.)* Shouldn't you be with your guests...Annetta?

ANNETTA: In a minute...guess I do have to go back... Mama can I talk to you a minute?

FLORIE: Solomon...why don't you go into your room for a few minutes.

SOLOMON: I don't feel like it. Don't come over here givin' orders like you still lived here. Go'n back next door where you belong.

FLORIE: Solomon! Hush your mouth! This is your sister you're talking to. Now go to your room...

(SOLOMON *stands crosses to wheelchair starts to wheel* BARTON *out,* FLORIE *crosses to stove pours cocoa.)*

ANNETTA: No! Leave him here! I want to…I have to talk to both of you.

SOLOMON: Can I go downstairs then?

FLORIE: Yes…but dress warm…

(SOLOMON *crosses left exits* BARTON *room.)*

ANNETTA: Mama…can I go into your room a minute…?

FLORIE: *(She crosses with spoon, napkin, cup right to* BARTON, *places cup on trunk, napkin under* BARTON *chin, spoon feeds him cocoa.)* What do you mean…my room? You act like this is no longer your house where you grew up….

ANNETTA: I feel like a stranger already Mama. Some parts of this…

(SOLOMON *enters from down stage room with coat and hat stands in arch way.)*

ANNETTA: …room seems like I've never seen them before…. *(She exits up stage room.)*

FLORIE: You be back within the hour!

SOLOMON: Yes ma'am. *(He crosses right to left of* BARTON.) She shouldn't have done it! She did this to him! *(He crosses up right center to apartment door crosses into hall, exits down steps to street.)*

FLORIE: Within the hour!

(FLORIE *goes over to* BARTON *and adjusts the blanket and back pillow. She feeds him cocoa.)*

FLORIE: Oh, I wish you could speak. I wish you could tell me it's all my fault. I tell myself over and over again but that's not enough. They'll all leave us soon… and it's going to be us. Get well, Joseph. Get well. I just didn't think…

(ANNETTA *enters from up stage room crosses to up center table.*)

FLORIE: ...at the time I was doing so wrong.

ANNETTA: Solomon's really mad at me...

FLORIE: He'll get over it.... He has to have time....

ANNETTA: Oh Mama...I don't know what to say....

FLORIE: Say what you have to, child.

ANNETTA: I am so sorry....

FLORIE: I don't think you can be sorry for being in love....

ANNETTA: That's just it...I don't know...I don't know if I know what love is. I only know I did this to Papa. I can't even look him in the eye.

FLORIE: Never blame yourself. It was me! You hear? Me! It was me who tried to let you experience (*She places cocoa on trunk.*) what I was too afraid to do myself... (*She crosses left to right of* ANNETTA.) ...it was me and your father knows it. It is me who will be responsible...

(EUSTACE *enters hall from* LIZZIE *apartment crosses left enter* BARTON *apartment with bottle and glass.*)

FLORIE: ...for all the unevenness of your road from here on in.

ANNETTA: No ! No! I knew what I was doing.

EUSTACE: There you are...

(FLORIE *crosses to left of* BARTON.)

EUSTACE: ...listen you got to come on over...we got folks over and they toastin' us...

ANNETTA: I'm busy now...can't you see?

EUSTACE: Listen...you think ain't nobody notice how y'all run out? All of y'all.... Ain't no Bartons over there....

ANNETTA: I'll be back over soon....

EUSTACE: You supposed to be there. You ain't a Barton no more.

FLORIE: Your husband is right...I'll go over... *(She takes napkin from* BARTON *chin crosses up center, places napkin in drain, crosses right, exits apartment, crosses right to* LIZZIE *door, exits.)* Annetta, remember...there's nothing wrong with your father's hearing.

(FLORIE goes.)

EUSTACE: Okay, baby...what's it gonna be...? You comin' or not?

ANNETTA: I can't... *(She sits stage left table chair.)* I don't feel comfortable with those people....

EUSTACE: What's wrong with 'em?

ANNETTA: I just don't...

EUSTACE: They're niggers...that it? They from the south...that it? Well let me tell you something. ...You a nigger now...just like your husband...just like you son gonna be... *(He crosses to left of* BARTON.*)* You hear that, old man? You gonna have a southern, nigger grandson...so you can just keep on staring with them eyes....

ANNETTA: "Those eyes."...

EUSTACE: What?

ANNETTA: Those eyes! Those eyes! Can't you speak correctly? He's staring with "those" eyes....

EUSTACE: So it starts, hunh? My talk was good enough for you on the roof...and it ain't about to change now. *(To* BARTON*)* You done this, old man. You put the poison in deep, but you ain't gonna win. I'm gonna have a baby and he gonna wipe your thinkin' clean. *(To* ANNETTA*)* Hot damn! We gotta get you from here. *(To* BARTON*)* From you! I see now we can't even live next door. That's too close. *(To* ANNETTA*)* Look at you! Look at him! He can't even talk and he still fillin' your mind with all that hockey. We gonna move. Even if it's gotta be as far as 61st Street. *(To* BARTON*)* I'm gonna have a baby and he ain't gonna be split in half. He gonna be whole...dammit! There ain't gonna be no north! No south! No east! No west! He just gonna be a nigger. You hear me? Just a nigger! *(To* ANNETTA*)* I guess it ain't full hit you yet, but I love you. Now, you pull yourself together. Say what you gotta say to him. Do what you gotta do and get what you gotta get, 'cause I want you back next door. 'Netta...this your husband talking.

(EUSTACE *turns and goes.* LIZZIE *comes out of her apartment.)*

LIZZIE: Oh...here you are! I was just comin' to get you.... This don't look right, you know. Y'all's the guest of honor...where's 'Netta?

EUSTACE: She's comin'!

(EUSTACE *and* LIZZIE *cross right exit to* LIZZIE's *apartment.)*

ANNETTA: Papa, what can I say? Can't you help me? I guess not. I guess nobody can help me now. I'm married. I thought I would be dancing through hoops on my wedding day, but I already start out feeling that I've done something wrong. You were right, I guess... 'cause things seem so different from what I thought they'd be. I shouldn't have done it but, I love him...I guess. Oh, Papa, I'm in it now and I can't get out. But one thing...Eustace is wrong. I am having a baby, but it's not going to be like he says. I'm never going to be far from you. When this baby is born, he's gonna be over here more than you can say. I want him to know you and love you...like I love you. I want him to be like you. Just like you.

(ANNETTA *kisses him and hurriedly runs out, slamming the door. We see her sadly going to* LIZZIE's *apartment.* BARTON *sits there for a few moments. Then suddenly, but with a little difficulty...he rises, his left side paralyzed. It is apparent that he has partially recovered from his stroke and has not informed his family. He looks toward heaven and smiles triumphantly.* NIMROD, *awakened by the slammed door, comes out of his bedroom, stares at him a moment and then, still unseen, goes back into his room...closing the door silently behind him.*)

END OF PLAY